Psychology Revivals

The Power of Mathematics

Originally published in 1964, *The Power of Mathematics* was written at a time when a rethinking of the role of mathematics in schools was being undertaken in many parts of the world, coupled in some centres with actual experimental work in the classroom.

In his first book *Building up Mathematics* Dr Dienes showed how, in the earlier stages of mathematics learning, the use of sufficiently varied apparatus can enable children to form their own mathematical concepts. This constructive phase is followed in due course – given the right conditions – by an analytic phase.

The Power of Mathematics gives detailed consideration to this more mature and highly productive phase in mathematics-learning. Helpful and stimulating at the time; all those engaged in education would value his refreshing comments on the nature of the learning process itself. Today it can be read in its historical context.

The Power of Mathematics

A Study of the Transition from the Constructive to the Analytical Phase of Mathematical Thinking in Children

Z. P. Dienes

Routledge
Taylor & Francis Group
LONDON AND NEW YORK

First published in 1964
by Hutchinson Educational

This edition first published in 2026 by Routledge
4 Park Square, Milton Park, Abingdon, Oxon, OX14 4RN

and by Routledge
605 Third Avenue, New York, NY 10158

Routledge is an imprint of the Taylor & Francis Group, an informa business

A Library of Congress record exists under LCCN: 64057939

ISBN: 978-1-041-34994-5 (hbk)
ISBN: 978-1-003-79550-6 (ebk)
ISBN: 978-1-041-34995-2 (pbk)

Book DOI 10.4324/9781003795506

The Power of Mathematics

A study of the transition from the constructive to the analytical phase of mathematical thinking in children

Z. P. DIENES
B.A., Ph.D.

Reader in Psychology
in the University of Adelaide

HUTCHINSON EDUCATIONAL

HUTCHINSON EDUCATIONAL LTD
178–202 Great Portland Street, London, W.1

London Melbourne Sydney
Auckland Bombay Toronto
Johannesburg New York

★

First published 1964

This book has been set in Times New Roman type face. It has been printed in Great Britain by The Anchor Press, Ltd., in Tiptree, Essex, on Antique Wove paper.

Contents

Preface

THE teaching of mathematics in schools is in a state of ferment today. Every country in the world is finding itself short of the scientists, technicians and other specialists needed to carry on a technological civilization. The bottleneck clearly lies in the education of young people. The basic skill underlying all scientific and technological skills is control of the tools of mathematical structures, and not enough young people even become aware of their existence. The majority of them go through school regarding mathematics as an arduous conditioning process which enables them to pass qualifying examinations for entry into the professions. A fundamental re-thinking of the role of mathematics in schools is therefore being undertaken in many parts of the world, coupled in some centres with actual experimental work in the classroom. In this way it is hoped to establish that radical changes are practicable, as well as economically desirable. It is certainly being found that exploration of the 'difficult' underlying mathematical structures, in place of the customary rote-learning of rules, delights rather than repels children. Any child, unless spoilt by long conditioning through extrinsic punishment-reward systems, will respond to a challenge that awakens his natural curiosity.

The re-thinking of mathematics-teaching can be classified under three headings:

(a) curriculum research,
(b) method research,
(c) fundamental research into the thought processes.

It is, of course, essential that theorizing on any of these topics should be accompanied by practical checking in the classroom. Such checking will tend to blur the hard and fast separation of the three categories, and the work needs to be both interdisciplinary and international.

The recent O.E.E.C. Seminar in France was an attempt to attack the problem in this way. A group of mathematicians and educationalists was instructed, as a result of this seminar, to make recommendations to the member countries about revised curricula, and to suggest possible teaching methods. The result was the revolutionary Dubrovnik Report.[1] This suggested that geometry-teaching should make use of the idea of the vector, in this way unifying algebraical and geometrical ideas. In algebra it recommends the introduction of groups, rings, fields and vector spaces. The general direction of teaching, it recommends, should be towards clarification of the axiomatic method, both in algebra and in geometry. *Abstractions* are to be derived by children from a great variety of *concrete* situations, involving the use of models and other physical aids as a basis for early learning. The ages at which such learning could usefully be introduced would need to be experimentally determined. For this reason the curricula are developed as sequences not necessarily tied to any particular age-groups.

Research projects into method have been progressing alongside these theoretical considerations. The most significant of these are probably the University of Illinois Arithmetic Project, the University of Illinois Committee on School Mathematics, the Syracuse University Madison Project and the Leicestershire Mathematics Project. The first three have, on the whole, used as their basis the class-discussion of common mathematical situations in symbolized form, and by this means it has proved possible to get young children interested in the structural aspects of these situations. Recently, however, members of UICSM have begun to emphasize the non-verbal aspects of mathematical insights and the dangers of premature verbalization.[2] The

[1] *Synopses for modern secondary school mathematics* O.E.E.C. Paris, 1961

[2] Gertrude Hendrix, 'Learning by Discovery' *The Mathematics Teacher* Vol. LIV. No. 5, May, 1961

Leicestershire Mathematics Project has, from its inception in 1958, emphasized the importance of preverbal mathematical thinking, and has used physical materials mathematically structured in such a way as to make it most probable that such preverbal thinking is initiated. The problems of passing from preverbal to fully symbolized forms of mathematical thinking are by no means few or easy. The first step towards the solution of any problem is awareness that it exists, and this is about as much as we appear to know for certain about the process of symbolization. The fifth chapter of this book outlines procedures that are likely to be successful or have already been found successful in the work of the Leicestershire Mathematics Project and elsewhere; the information given is to be regarded as a pointer to the truth rather than a solid body of established fact.

Fundamental research has been carried out in Geneva under the direction of the well-known Swiss psychologist Jean Piaget, and more recently at the Harvard University Center for Cognitive Studies under the direction of Jerome Bruner. These studies are still only in their initial stages but provide useful indications.

My own proposals implicitly assume the correctness of the pioneering work of the Geneva school and explicitly build upon the preliminary findings of the Harvard Center and the theoretical work previously done by me at Leicester University. The subject-matter covered, although of necessity a small fraction of what might be done in schools, is in line with the recommendations of the Dubrovnik Report. The suggestions contained in the second chapter, on how children might learn powers, roots and logarithms, have stemmed from my recent work at the Harvard Center, and have been included partly as an illustration of the theory of mathematics-learning developed there, and partly to bring home to teachers that children's ability to meet serious mathematical challenges at a remarkably early age has been underestimated. The work on powers, roots and logarithms was first done with intelligent nine-year-olds, who thoroughly enjoyed the sessions. It is not suggested that there is any virtue in pushing the syllabus down to younger and younger age-groups; but if children are not intellectually challenged they soon become bored and their interest fades away. It is the lack of challenge in our present syllabuses which may be responsibile in part for the dislike of, or, at best, indifference towards, mathematics which is all too prevalent in schools.

Again in line with the recommendations of the Dubrovnik Report, the last chapter deals with ways in which axiomatic methods can be introduced. It may be found that the analysis of the steps leading from statement to statement in a proof is too difficult in the beginning. Such an analysis does, in the last resort, imply a logical analysis of methods of thinking, and children in schools may not be mature enough to reflect on their own reflections. It may be possible, however, to alter this state of affairs by the early introduction of logic as a subject of study, and later formulation of its rules in symbolized form. The introduction of set theoretical notions has already been tried successfully in some schools in the United States from the fourth grade up (through the School Mathematics Study Group, directed by Professor Begle) and even in the first grade in some Palo Alto schools (tried out by Suppes). As set theoretical operations correspond exactly to logical operations, a bridgehead has already been established for the study of logic in schools. How this study will eventually tie up with the use of the axiomatic method is for future research to determine, but work is in progress and results may be expected within the next few years.

The theoretical and practical expositions that follow are the result of much painstaking work, a great deal of it done in classes of over forty children working sometimes under indifferent physical conditions. The author's gratitude is expressed to the hundreds of teachers, and literally thousands of children, without whose enthusiastic co-operation the work on which this volume is based could never have been done.

Adelaide, 1963 Z.P.D.

Introduction

IN A previous book[1] I have tried to indicate how mathematics can be built up almost entirely through constructive thought processes in the early stages. These stages approximately correspond to the Junior School years, and a great number of Junior teachers in different parts of the world have discovered from experience that during these years a considerable amount of serious mathematics may be learnt by children, provided they are given the appropriate experiences. In my book I described a number of examples of how to construct systematic series of situations of this nature. This stock of experiences provides a kind of mathematical capital, which serves children in good stead when they need to become fully aware of what they have constructed. The 'becoming aware' stage is really the analytical aspect of the mathematics with which they have become familiar as constructions only. This present book will be largely concerned with the transition from the predominantly constructive to the more analytical or logical stage, and to some extent with the development of the analytical processes and the role of a growing symbolism.

The transition from the constructive stage is usually heralded by 'Why?' questions. Suppose that children have been building up towards the factorization of $A^2 + 2AB + B^2$, and that they have realized the following:

If you set out a number of equal groups of things so that there are two more groups than there are things in each group and put one more thing to these, the total of these things can always be arranged into exactly as many groups as there are things in a group. In each such group there will

[1] *Building up mathematics* Hutchinson, London, 1960

be one more thing than before, and there will be one less group. This can always be done (or so it seems), whatever the size of the groups that you start with.

When children do these exercises and see that, whatever size group they start with, the 'pattern' is always the same, *sometimes* they begin to wonder why this is so. Many children, convinced by the repetition of the same pattern, are ready to believe that it must obviously continue, in a world made up of all sorts of regularities which you find out about by observation. But others go beyond this point, not so much because they are in any doubt about the working of the rule, but because they are curious to know why it works that way and not another way. After all, why do you not get two more objects in the transformed collections, why always one more? The appearance of such enquiries ushers in the analytical stage, the stage of 'Why?' and 'What is it made of?' and 'Could you have it another way if you changed it a little?' and so on.

What kind of help, then, can a teacher provide for a child who is asking questions of this kind, particularly if the child is not yet familiar with the properties of the accompanying mathematical symbolism? It can be suggested, in the example just given, that a method of transforming the groups he found can be done by the least number of transfers of objects from group to group. This often results in the realization that if one whole group is emptied it yields enough objects for adding one object to all the remaining groups but one. The extra object will complete the deficient group. Realization of why this works still may not follow, but can be encouraged by splitting the groups into two parts: two groups in one part, and the remainder of the groups in another, as on the opposite page.

The crucial point is that the number of objects in the larger group of groups is bound to be the same as the number of objects in each group. Therefore one such group—for example, one of the two in the first part—can be emptied, and there is *bound to be* one object each which can

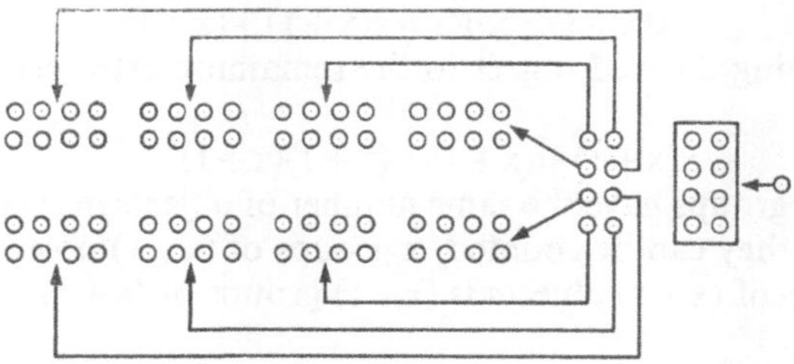

be added to the groups in the second part. The extra object is added to the extra group that is left.

The 'reason' why this transformation of groups always works is in the relationship between the number of groups and the number of objects in each group. The first extra group is distributed among the rest. There is one more group that gets no object in this way, and this group gets the extra one. The compelling necessity of this never-failing situation is then translated into the *symbolic* transformation

$$(x+2)\,x+1=(x+1)\,(x+1)$$

where x denotes the number of objects in a group before we transformed them. The number of groups originally is $(x+2)$, after the transformation it is $(x+1)$, i.e. one less than before. The number of objects in one of the final groups is also $(x+1)$, this is on the other hand one more than before.

The symbolic equivalent of the whole series of steps that provide the 'reason' for the identity above would go as follows:

$$(x+2)x+1=x^2+2x+1$$
(splitting of groups into two parts)

$$x^2+2x+1=x^2+x+x+1$$
(separating of the two odd groups)

$$x^2+x+x+1=x(x+1)+x+1$$
(emptying one group and joining objects to x other groups)

$$x(x+1)+x+1=x(x+1)+(x+1)$$

(joining the odd object to the remaining extra group)

$$x(x+1)+(x+1)=(x+1)(x+1)$$

(all the groups have the same number of objects in them now and so they can be counted, x groups of (x+1) objects plus 1 group of (x+1) objects is (x+1) groups of (x+1) objects)

It will be clear that the substance of the argument is psychologically speaking quite a different thing from the symbolic or formal deduction of the identity. If the two are not joined in one mental process the activity is not really complete. The manipulation of the mathematical signs without the accompanying meaning comes close to being a kind of mental juggling. On the other hand, carrying out transformations without the help of symbols very soon leads into an impasse, because we cannot keep in mind, let alone process, the infomation needed to effect further transformations.

Any teacher who is content to let his students go on carrying out more and more complicated transformations in the formal way, without making sure that *at any stage* the corresponding reality could be experienced by them, is not going to find much in this volume to his liking. It is not, of course, suggested that every single transformation must be thought out and translated into corresponding transformations of groups of objects. This is no more necessary than being aware of where we put our feet every time we go up and down stairs. The stairs are familiar and we have worked out once and for all how to solve the problems of locomotion up and down them. In the same way we can work out how to find our way about mathematical structures quite mechanically. But it should be possible to revert to first principles if need be: for example, if we are picking our way through a treacherous marsh every footstep needs to be carefully considered, and the awareness of our activity is greatly heightened. Corresponding increases in awareness in mathematical work should occur every time we begin to tread on unfamiliar mathematical ground, as the pitfalls of erroneous mathematical thinking are many, and no mechanical set of rules will cater for all of them. To make sure that this increase of awareness is possible whenever it is needed, the learning process must be carefully planned so that children learn the necessary mathematical intricacies through becoming aware of them for themselves. This book will therefore be devoted largely to explaining how, once mathematical constructions have been built up, their functioning may be appreciated by children in every detail.

I

How Mathematics is Learnt

IT IS very daring to ask ourselves to explain how mathematics is learnt. In fact it is somewhat daring to ask how anything at all is learnt, once we depart from the stimulus-response explanation, which is really no explanation at all but merely the statement of the fact that things appear to be learnt when certain conditions are satisfied. We may well ask ourselves the more fundamental question, of what does learning really consist? If we say that something has been learnt when the same situation is handled more effectively after than before learning, even if we could find an adequate way of measuring the effectiveness of handling situations, we should still be stating certain relevant facts about learning rather than explaining how learning takes place. If we think about the matter a little more we might be tempted to think that there is no way of 'explaining' learning in terms of observed facts only, as in fact there is no way of 'explaining' any complex phenomenon in terms of observed facts only. To explain a phenomenon is surely to suggest a framework which would in some way tidy up the facts observed, make it possible to see them as a whole pattern, so that by working the pattern we can predict what might happen next.

This is what happens in any science when a theory is proposed or used; the theory is a proposed co-ordinator of observed facts in terms of which we can 'make sense' of the facts, as we might say, and so predict future events. If our predictions are on the whole validated, we can say that our theory works. If the theory has poor predictive value, then it does not work very well, it is like a suit of clothes that does not fit the wearer; in such cases we look around for a theory, or suit of clothes, that will fit the facts, or ourselves, as the case may be, more efficiently. What we cannot say about any theory is that it is true, neither can we say that it is false. It either works or it does not. If it works, we use it; if it does not, we reject it. A theory could go on working quite well for quite a long time, in the sense of providing accurate predictions in terms of the events we are considering. New classes of relevant events which might come to light often upset a theory. This is no tragedy, it merely means we have grown out of the theory and it is time to look around for a new one. It is extremely important to make a careful distinction between statements about facts, which are verifiable by direct reference to the facts in question, and statements about theoretical models in terms of which facts are 'explained' or made to 'make sense' to us; the latter are essentially unverifiable as such, since these models have no factual existence. We cannot say that it is a fact that the force of gravity makes an apple fall to the ground when it is severed from the tree. We can only verify that the apple falls, not that some mysterious thing called gravity 'makes it fall'. Such formulations of explanations are the remnants of our animistic past. Gravity no more makes the apple fall than a differential equation keeps the Sydney Harbour Bridge from falling down. Each fact fits into a set of other facts which are held in some sort of tidy arrangement—in one case by a theory of gravitation, in the other by the satisfaction of some differential equations which keep the operating stresses and strains in stable equilibrium. But I see I have slipped into the very error for which I was chiding the general public. It is not the differential equations that *keep* the stresses and strains in equilibrium, it is from the properties of these equations that I can predict that if I build a certain type of structure, then the real stresses and strains will remain in a real stable equilibrium. So it is with any learning theory we or anyone else might propose.

The sense-impressions that impinge upon our sense-organs during a lifetime are very numerous and very varied.

Yet we must sort out these impressions somehow so that we can find our way about in this extremely complex phenomenal environment. A puff of smoke on the horizon at sea would indicate to most people the presence of a ship (although it could be a volcanic island appearing out of the sea at a great distance), a puff of smoke behind a chair would indicate that somebody was smoking a cigarette or pipe (although it might be the start of a fire caused by a spark from the fireplace). We seem to learn to associate certain cues with certain phenomena, and the presence of these cues in certain given circumstances induces us to believe that certain events are happening or are about to happen. And we are nearly always right. In this way events are sorted out into classes, even though the same cue might under different circumstances mean different events, and the same events might be predicted by a variety of different cues. The classes 'ship', 'person smoking', etc., are useful classes, as we can use them to sort out our environment and make sense of it. This sorting out of events into classes is a fundamental process, part of the process of adaption to the environment. It is followed by the realization of the relationships between the classes formed. It is through the manipulation of such relationships that we make predictions. For example there is a close relationship between the West Coast of Scotland and rainfall. By being aware of this relationship we can predict considerable rain on a proposed holiday on the West Coast of Scotland, and we make sure that every member of the family has a good raincoat. The relationships that we handle daily are of not much greater complexity and the class relationships of (i) inclusion; (ii) identity; (iii) distinctness; (iv) overlapping; together with the element-class relationship at one level, are usually sufficient for us to cope with most situations in life. For example, if a Hungarian wanted to go to New Guinea as a missionary he would realize that the classes of Hungarian speakers and New Guinea natives were entirely distinct. He would deduce that he would have to learn a language other than Hungarian. When we say of a boy that he must have or have had some parents, we are implying the identity of the class of all males and the class of all sons. When we say that a young person of 18 may go into a public house and partake of an alcoholic beverage we are saying that the class of 18-year-olds is included in the class of people allowed alcoholic beverages in public houses. To make use of these relationships it is necessary for us to be at least implicitly aware of the properties of such relationships, as well as able to recognize exemplars *and* non-exemplars of the relevant classes whenever we come across them. These conditions are not always met, resulting in what may be termed 'muddled thinking'. For example a conversation might run like this:

A. 'I think all foreigners are dishonest!'

B. 'But you said Mr Smith was a cheat, and he's not a foreigner!'

B clearly confuses two opposite inclusions. A implies by what he says that:

The class of foreigners is included in *the class of dishonest people.*

Mr Smith can well be a cheat for all that, without being a foreigner as, according to A at least, the class of dishonest people includes foreigners and possibly many others, and so quite possibly Mr Smith. He is certainly not contradicting himself. B of course has understood A to have said that:

The class of dishonest people is included in *the class of foreigners,*

i.e. that all dishonest people are foreigners. This would indeed exclude Mr Smith from the possibility of being a cheat, were the assertion true. B confuses an inclusion with the inverted inclusion and imputes illogicality to A of which he is guilty himself. All this of course quite irrespective of whether the statements are true or false in fact.

B was clearly unaware of the non-invertibility of an inclusion (or implication) statement. When negations (i.e. complements of classes) are introduced, the situation tends to get even more muddled. The fact that the world is not a more confused place than it is seems to indicate that the great majority of situations that the great majority of people have to deal with are really extremely simple.

Now mathematical thinking not only deals with the sorting out of mathematical classes and the realization of what these classes have to do with each other. It extends the element-class relationship by considering the newly formed classes to be elements of further classes, these classes again as elements of yet further classes and so on. In other words the *level* of the element-class relationship shifts, as do the elements and the classes themselves. To take a non-mathematical example, the class of chairs has for its elements chairs, i.e. objects of a certain type of construction. When we say or write 'chair' we do not necessarily mean any particular chair, unless we specify it by saying 'this chair', or 'the green wing chair in the large bedroom' or something like that. So 'chair' is no longer an object, it is a class of objects for which the symbol in the English language is the word 'chair'. We form a great number of such classes, all of which are denoted by a word. These words form the class of concrete nouns, of which the elements are no longer objects but classes of objects. We have therefore raised the element-class relationship to the next level. A noun (adjective, verb, conjunction, etc.) would be described as a 'part of speech', a class of which 'noun', 'adjective', etc., would be the elements. This again induces a shift to the next level. Mathematical thinking abounds in such shifts, where superstructures are constantly being built on what has been built before.

The shift of level here referred to is not to be confused with class-inclusions like class of chairs included in class of furniture; it is an actual *chair* which is a piece of furniture, not the class of chairs. In other words, element to class relationship (i.e. belonging) is not the same as class to class relationship (i.e. inclusion).

Learning anything new, and in particular learning mathematics, consists of

(i) sorting events into classes or categories, so that any event is immediately recognized as either belonging or not belonging to a class or category, or of course as being irrelevant to it;

(ii) becoming aware of the relationship to each other of the classes or categories constructed.

But how are we to be satisfied that a person has formed a particular class or category? We might say that the class 'red' has been learnt if a person invariably selects a red object from a selection of coloured objects when he is asked to select a red object. One must, of course, be reasonably certain that the subject is co-operating, and where human behaviour is concerned we can hardly ever speak of 100 per cent certainty. The only part of the sequence of events leading to the statement 'A has formed the class of red objects' which is verifiable is whether A does or does not pick red objects when called upon to do so. When we say that *therefore* he has learnt about red (just because we have seen him picking out red objects), we are doing no more than manipulate a model, a theory. It would be reasonably certain that a successful performance with coloured counters would enable someone to learn to stop at traffic lights when they turn red. This is a prediction which the model, however simple, has enabled us to make. However, it is not learning of the class 'red' that makes him eventually stop at the red lights, but various neural connexions that have been established as a result of past experiences.

The fundamental question that interests the psychologist who is working on Cognition is just how regularities are discovered in the environment. But what, in any case, do we mean by 'discovering' regularities? The world of objective reality consists of an enormous number of particles moving about with all sorts of speeds and accelerations. When we speak of regularity, we refer to our evaluation of the sense-impressions presented to our senses by these seething masses of atoms and electrons. It is difficult to see how any essentially objective regularity could exist. Yet the fact is that we have an inveterate tendency to sort things out into regular patterns, and indeed the Gestalt psychologists insist that this is a tendency built into the human organism. Certainly the ability to see things in regularly recurring patterns has great survival value. A certain kind of roar or smell indicated to our forefathers the presence of a dangerous animal, and led to immediate scaling of a tree in consequence. If every roar were regarded as a separate event, and not as a member of a class of dangerous roars, the chances of survival would obviously be very small in a jungle full of carnivores.

Before we have sorted something out, it appears to us as a puzzle. What do we do with a puzzle? Generally the first thing is some seemingly random 'fiddling about'. We may try to fit this here and that there and see what happens. If we have no inhibitions about the sort of thing we must not do, our attempts will range over an open field—we shall be getting the feel of the puzzle. When we move to a new town, unless we have studied the town map beforehand, the whole place will seem a jumble of houses, streets, traffic lights, signposts, street signs, etc. We may spend quite a time wandering about the town, on foot or driving, getting generally familiar with it. Gradually the sequences of cues will coalesce into a whole pattern, and we shall eventually be able to find our way from any part of the town to any other part without asking for directions. (The reader might have noticed that this tends not to happen if he is driven everywhere by friends.) The traffic system and general street-structure of the town will become clear to us. This knowledge, which is not just an agglomeration of facts but also their co-ordination into a coherent picture, will be our guide on any future journeys through the town. Now how did this happy state of affairs come about? By what we might term 'exploring' the town. We have manipulated the data, namely the streets and the cues to be seen on and around them, possibly quite randomly, possibly for quite other reasons than getting to know the town. Such manipulation has given us the 'cognitive map' of the town; it is so with any *natural* acquisition of knowledge, whether it be a motor skill like skating or riding a bicycle or an intellectual skill like learning a language.

We must consider for a moment the difference between *natural* and *artificial* learning, for this provides important clues to the understanding of children's difficulties when they are confronted with artificial scholastic learning situations. If a child is taken to a foreign country where his mother-tongue is not spoken, within a few months he can speak the new language as well as his newly acquired friends, whereas his parents may still be struggling with grammar years later, trying to learn the language 'properly'. It is, of course, the child who has learnt it 'properly', and the reason is that he has learnt it naturally. Fortunately it is impossible to learn skating or riding a bicycle from a book, or many people would have a try. The 'fiddling around' with the data is the only way of making sure that you do not eventually take a tumble on the ice or fall off your bicycle. Natural learning is not invariably preferable to artificial learning; it is however *a priori* probable that it will be more effective. Previous study of the plan of our new town would no doubt accelerate the natural process of getting to know its structure, although it is difficult to believe that exclusive study of it would make a person just as confident in finding his way about as an inhabitant of several years' standing.

Fortunately for children and teachers, much mathematical 'fiddling around' takes place in the nursery before a child goes to school. He plays with objects and sorts them into groups. He is bound to establish the idea of 'two' from his experiences. Ideas such as 'the same as', 'greater than' and 'smaller than' are also required in sorting out playthings or comparing his parents and brothers and sisters or friends. These ideas will not mean just the same for the child as they do for the adult. The classic work of Piaget shows that children do not regard equally numerous collections of objects as 'the same' if one collection is more scattered and takes up more room than the other. Nevertheless the child evolves classifications of his own, and for his purposes they work very well. Nobody teaches him these things. It is his ordering of the chaos around him, it is natural learning.

Civilized life, however, requires certain skills that are not acquired in the natural course of events. These have therefore had to be *taught* to those who need them. The handing down of manual skills from father to son might still be considered a fairly natural process, in the sense that it would be part of the child's natural adaptation to the home environment to try to imitate his father. This process of learning has been somewhat formalized but kept in essentials in the system of apprenticeship. It is a kind of soaking-in process, of which the pupils are hardly aware. The institutions where learning has become most artificial are the schools. Adult society, often quite irrationally, decides what the next generation ought to learn, and this is made into the contents of syllabuses. Apart from the vague reasons advanced for the inclusion of this or that subject-matter—the result of much muddled thinking and outworn prejudice—there is serious neglect of the study of the learning process itself. There has never been in any country a systematic programme of research. We have scratched a little on the surface of the problem by comparative studies of teaching method, and by simplified analysis of the learning process in the laboratory. But the study of method leaves us in the dark about how the process of learning really takes place; and the study of the reactions of rats in mazes or of human beings learning nonsense syllables or artificial Chinese characters[1] is unlikely to be applicable to the enormously more complex learning and much more complex social situation found in real schools.

At any rate, the artificial learning now taken for granted in the mathematics lesson does entail a very large failure rate. There is a virtual lack of understanding of the mathematical structures. In the large majority of cases, what students communicate by writing down or uttering mathematical signs is merely the signs themselves and not the structures for which the signs are supposed to act as symbols. This is like learning the phonetic structure and

[1] Hull, C. L., 'Quantitative aspects of the evolution of concepts; an experimental study' *Psychol. Monogr.* (1920) Vol. 28, No. 123

orthography of a language, and being able to read aloud anything written in that language, without understanding what it is intended to convey. One way of overcoming this has been demonstrated by the Leicestershire Mathematics Project, reported in my earlier book.[1] In this project, mathematical situations were set up from which children learned mathematical structures in much the same way as they learn about structures in the real world; that is, by manipulating actual objects. Most of this is done at the constructive level, i.e. at the level of constructing classes out of seemingly unconnected events. But a stage is inevitably reached in the learning of complex structures when we must begin to be fully aware of the properties of the constructions that we have made, or we cannot proceed any further. We must double back on our tracks and see how we arrived where we are. To think about what has been done is a more sophisticated activity than the mere doing of it. It is also a more mature activity. This kind of activity only comes to full maturity during the teenage years, although of course it is observable earlier in more rudimentary forms. It is an analytical activity, as opposed to the previous constructive activity. Construction has to precede analysis, or there would be nothing to analyse. Equally there must be some material out of which to make the original construction, or there would be nothing to construct. This material is, first, the basic elements out of which classes are constructed and, second, the classes themselves out of which yet higher-order classes are formed.

We have seen that the process often, if not always, takes place as a result of seemingly random activity, referred to as 'fiddling round' or perhaps more aptly as 'playing around'. It is essentially the same process that a child must go through when familiarizing himself with the feel of building bricks, getting used to their behaviour in a constant gravitational field with the frictional force between the surfaces remaining between certain limits. The limitations of the material automatically limit the kind of things you can do with it. For

[1] *Building up mathematics*

example, it is impossible to balance a building brick along one of its edges without leaning it against something else. The playing child does not become explicitly aware of the possibilities and prohibitions, but with a great deal of random playing around behind him he gathers an implicit knowledge of what is possible. The class of 'possible structures that can be built with building bricks' gradually takes shape, including sub-classifications such as 'possible towers', 'possible walls', 'possible tunnels', etc. It is amazing how effectively a child can wield these classes, pragmatically, without being at all aware of the relationships of the classes with which he is working. He will know how to build a certain type of building without analysing his actions. He knows what he wants to make, and he goes and makes it. This is essentially constructive activity, and the constructions are essentially the result of manipulative play with available material. This is true whether the material consists of objects that can be handled or of classes of objects that are already abstractions. A two- to three-year-old child can handle the mathematical concept of 'two' in practical situations. But this concept is already on the second level of class-formation! The number 'two' is not a property of objects; it is a property of collections, of classes of objects. Of all the collections of objects, pairs of objects possess the property of there being two objects in the collection. Yet the young child is able to handle such a double-storey construction with the greatest of ease and without any formal teaching. He has constructed his 'two', his 'three', etc., out of his own manipulation of the world around him.

Learning appears to take the course of plunging headlong into a mass of seemingly disconnected phenomena, and by interfering with these phenomena, by getting the feel of how to induce the happening of certain desired phenomena, to formulate the properties of different sorts of environments in terms of certain rules. The rules are the properties that events must have in order to fall into a certain class; for example, towers must not be leaning too far or they will collapse. The event of producing a tower cannot take place if the necessary properties of the bricks are not observed. The rules are a restriction on what is possible, yet the realization of the rules gives a new freedom of action, for it enables us to predict effectively what we shall be able to do. An engineer can plan the boring of a tunnel under Mont Blanc or the English Channel because he can handle the rule-structures, in terms of which he can predict what will happen if certain things are done. He plays by the rules. This is quite a different kind of 'play' from the manipulative play which induced us to discover or formulate the rules in the first place. We now have a powerful and sophisticated tool which we can wield and enjoy.

Let us now see whether anything comparable takes place in the classroom. Where do we find the sorting out of experience into rule-structures, and the subsequent use of such structures? There are isolated centres where learning in this 'natural' way is being tried, but they are few and far between. Past attempts, such as those of Maria Montessori, have not spread because they had been based on one brilliant teacher's intuition, and the underlying rationale has never been thoroughly investigated. Reasonably enough, attempts to alter the learning situation radically in schools have been opposed by both administrators and teachers. Before it becomes possible to convince educational authorities of the need for change, successful pilot experiments must take place. A working theory, applicable to the average and not merely the exceptional classroom, is essential.

We must therefore take our consideration of the learning process a stage further. Let us assume that, through random manipulation, we have arrived at the construction of a class or classes. Of course the manipulation is not uniformly random throughout the process. It becomes less and less random, i.e. more and more purposeful, as possible useful classifications occur to us. These are put to the test consciously or instinctively and thus confirmed or rejected, until a final and workable structure emerges. For example, children at first nearly always confuse odd numbers and prime numbers, as they do square numbers and even numbers. The number 39 is invariably considered prime, possibly because it is not in the usual multiplication tables, or simply because, being odd, it is regarded as a safe candidate for primehood. Squares have four corners, and so how could 9 possibly be a square when it is odd? This is the kind of idea that mills around in a child's head before he has sorted out the mathematical classes and their relationships. It is a delicate transition stage, and to criticize such ideas as 'absurd' will clearly not help the child to sort the matter out. Examples or counter-examples can be suggested to him, to provide additional data through which he can reach his conclusions. Once these conclusions have been arrived at, the rule-structure is ready for 'playing with', instead of 'playing towards'. In the case of prime numbers and squares, a useful relationship to work on is this: a prime that is the sum of two squares, when divided by 4, leaves remainder 1; conversely a prime that when divided by 4 leaves remainder 1 is the sum of two squares. In other words, there is an identity relationship between the two classes: 'Primes which are sums of two squares' and 'Primes which when divided by 4 leave remainder 1'. Children will find an exhilarating sense of power as they sort out all the classes involved. There are (a) even numbers; (b) odd numbers; (c) prime numbers; (d) numbers that are sums of two squares; (e) numbers that when you divide by 4 leave remainder 1. On this basis our identity relationship becomes:

The common part of (c) and (e) = The common part of (c) and (d).

Negations of class-properties lead to complementary classes. If we use N for the negation of a property, we could denote all 'numbers that are not even' by N(a). We have two obvious class-identities:

N(a) = (b) and N(b) = (a)

or again:

The common part of (a) and (c) = The class consisting of the number 2, written as (2).

Or we can concentrate on class-inclusions such as:

The joint class (b) and (2) includes (c)

There is no question at this stage of 'proving' class-identities or inclusions. The necessity for such 'proofs' will arise naturally out of playing by the rules. This, however, is already the harbinger of another stage.

There appear to be at least three paths that we can take from the stage of rule-bound play. The simplest is to become so familiar with what we are playing with that we cease to think about it; somehow the structure soaks into us as one more method of sorting out aspects of our environment. We might call this the path of *practice*. By it we eventually reach the stage when we can recognize an actual situation as being relevant (or not relevant) in relation to the rules we have learnt. Suppose we have had some exercises to lead us to appreciate the structure of positive and negative numbers. When we come across situations involving rises and falls of temperature, increasing and decreasing speeds, displacements in two opposite directions, etc., we recognize these as situations in which the use of positive and negative numbers is relevant. Unfortunately, if the exercises have not done their work properly, we shall 'recognize' situations as relevant even when they are not. If we ask someone who has been learning about negative numbers how many books there will be on the table if from the two books there we remove three, he might in all seriousness tell us that there would be minus-one book on the table. He might have second thoughts if we required him to carry out the operation and show us the minus-one book left on the table! Even then, he might not realize that the situation of the books on the table is simply not relevant to directed numbers. It is amazing how people disregard common sense, once they start to learn what they believe to be mathematics. In this case, practice in applying the structure of directed numbers to relevant situations, and in rejecting it with irrelevant situations, will eventually make the structure operational, without yielding any deep insight into its details or the internal relationships of which it is composed.

Another path we might take is to examine how the rules function, how they are related to each other. This is looking back on what we have done, in a critical, analytical way. We could call it *retroactive analysis*. As in our example we quickly realize that, in the structure known as the algebra of directed numbers, to every number there is an 'opposite' number (e.g. 3 is opposite to -3, -6 is opposite to 6, etc.), what we might fail to realize is that adding a number is completely equivalent to subtracting the opposite number, and subtracting a number is completely equivalent to adding the opposite number, although in fact we carry out these operations correctly every time.[1] But by going back and examining what we have been doing, we become aware of a certain regularity. This is retroactive analysis. When we merely practise the rules and the rules soak into our bones, we become less rather than more aware of them. When we go back and examine what we have been doing, we are consciously attempting to become aware of the relationships that make the learnt rule-structure what it is. Practice is a less conscious, analysis a more conscious, activity.

There is yet another, more adventurous way of handling the learning of a rule-structure. If we have played with our rule-structure and examined it in detail, we may have found it wanting in certain respects. So we might either alter the rules, or at any rate extend them. This is *progressive analysis*, and any extension of the rule-structure is referred to as *generalization*. For example, we might realize that directed numbers only allow the variation of one variable in one of two opposing senses, whereas most situations in

[1] For example see David Page's games with 'negative' money

life require more than one variable to describe them. If we want to give the position of a ship at sea, we need to specify longitude as well as latitude. The two variables are independent, in the sense that on the open sea we can vary one without varying the other (i.e. for example we can sail entirely due East, or entirely due South) or we can vary both quite independently of each other (i.e. we can sail from a given spot on the ocean in any direction we see fit). If we also want to specify air-temperature, water-temperature, air-pressure, relative humidity, and the time at which all these readings are taken, we are dealing with seven variables. Considerations of this kind would lead us away from a one-dimensional space of directed numbers to a *generalization*, that is, a 7-dimensional space based on states or vectors. Such a generalization is essentially an extension of a class with a known structure to another more extensive class, of which the previous structure is but a special case. Generalization is not to be confused with abstraction, which is the formation of a class directly from elements. The directed numbers themselves are the elements of the class of directed numbers; the states or vectors are the elements of the class of multi-dimensional vectors. But the *class* of directed numbers is not an element of the *class* of multi-dimensional vectors. We have to be careful not to confuse class-inclusion or class-extension with the notion of being an element of, or belonging to, a class. The formation of a class out of elements is essentially the abstraction process, whereas the extension of an already existing class into a more extensive class is the generalization process.[1]

Instead of merely extending the rule-structure, it is possible to decree an alteration of the rule-structure. After all, rules are there to serve us, not bind us. If we can find other rules which serve us better, we might alter the rules. This is what happens when a new theory is proposed. Such revolutionary thinking might occur more often in

[1] Dienes, Z. P., 'On abstraction and generalization' *Harvard Educational Review*, Summer, 1961

adults if children were trained to be more audacious. Our present educational practices induce a high order of conformity, and it is often the slightly unbalanced people who dare to upset the established rule-structure. To train our children to think in revolutionary ways might indeed have revolutionary results—not a bad thing in the state of the world today!

Let us come back to the process under investigation. We have practised, analysed or generalized the rule-structures which we previously moulded out of the chaos of our sense-impressions through manipulative play. We are now thoroughly familiar with these structures. Are we not once again in the position in which we were when we started, except that we now have more things to play with? The new structures are the new playthings. Of course we are not yet familiar with the *relationships between* our new toys, only with the internal structure of each toy. To get the feel of how the new toys can be played with, we have to start again the whole process of manipulations. We have turned a full circle, or rather a spiral, since we are on a higher level than we were before. We are starting out on a new *cycle*, trying this and that, seeing how the new toys will fit, how they will not fit, and generally moving towards the undiscovered rule-structure that governs the new toys. Eventually this cycle, too, will come to a conclusion, and in this way a succession of new structures can be built up by mathematicians.

It is this working through cycles that I have called elsewhere the *application* of the dynamic principle. In my formulation of the principle, construction precedes and leads into analysis (which was previously regarded as a separate principle). Both principles are incorporated into a new and fuller dynamic principle.

It is time now to consider in a little more detail how the cycles run, and what the circumstances are that make them run more (or less) efficiently. What makes for more rapid, more effective abstraction? In other words, how should we set up a situation in which we might expect classes to be formed rapidly and effectively? First, we need to decide the class or classes we wish our pupils to form. Problems must then be devised which will ensure that

(a) future situations will be recognized as relevant or irrelevant in relation to the abstraction required;
(b) in the situations correctly judged as relevant, exemplars of classes will be recognized as belonging to the classes in question; non-exemplars as not so belonging.

To satisfy the first condition, a kind of mental sieve must be constructed into which situations are placed, the irrelevant ones passing through the sieve, the relevant ones retained. This is no easy business. How did Newton realize that objects *falling* towards the earth, and the moon travelling round the earth in an orbit and *not falling* towards it, formed part of a useful class of events? He considered that objects were being *attracted* towards each other. In the first case the objects were the falling object and the earth, in the second case the moon and the earth. This 'attraction' is merely a manner of speech by which the two events are put in the same category; through such categorizing, better and more accurate predictions become possible. All classifications are abstractions, not realities. They help to sort out realities, but they are not realities themselves. Newton managed to extract something valid which two situations had in common. This he achieved by looking at these situations from a number of different angles, some of them unusual for his time. Perhaps achieving an abstraction, i.e. formulating a regularity, is the result of looking at events from a large number of different angles. How can we translate this into practice during the mathematics lesson? Since mathematical 'events' hardly ever happen naturally in children's experience, we must make them happen. The mathematical structures which we expect our children to acquire as their stock-in-trade should be presented to them in different embodiments; that is, the children should encounter the same mathematical structure dressed up in a number of ways.

A child learning to recognize the situations in which quadratic functions are involved might be led to recognize the following two as *relevant*:

'As many tanks go into battle as the number of each tank-crew. One tank gets a direct hit and everyone is killed in it. Six more soldiers are lost out of the rest of the force. At the end of the battle, they find some abandoned enemy tanks. They find that they can bring back to their own lines their own remaining tanks as well as the enemy ones with equal crews, but of course depleted ones. By how many people is each crew depleted, and how many enemy tanks did they capture?'

'Make a square on a pegboard out of a large number of pegs. Then remove one row of your square, and any other six pegs from the board. Make a rectangle out of the remaining pegs. How many more or less rows will your rectangle have than your square had, and how many more or less pegs will there be in each of these rows than in a row of the square?'

In fact these examples are not merely relevant to quadratic functions, they are from the mathematical point of view the identical problem. The realization of this identity entails the ability to discard irrelevancies and retain essentials. The mathematical relevance lies in the number relationships in the problems, not in the 'dressing up'. The 'as many tanks as the number of the crew in each tank' corresponds to the square of pegs, through 'as many rows of pegs as there are pegs in each row'. The rows correspond to the tanks, and the pegs to the soldiers. The direct hit on one tank corresponds to the removal of one row, the six others that die correspond to the six other pegs that are removed. The sorting out of the remaining force into equal groups corresponds to the sorting out of the remaining pegs into a larger number of rows than before with each row being shorter than before. The number less in each row corresponds to the number by which each crew is depleted, and so on. Such correspondence will help to get children to realize what the mathematical aspect of the problem is, as opposed to the 'real situation' aspect. The mathematical aspect is that which has been abstracted from a number of different situations.

In addition to recognizing relevance and irrelevance, it is necessary to recognize exemplars and non-exemplars. The above two examples are exemplars of the use of factors of quadratic functions for the purpose of achieving the solution of a whole class of problems. But what about recognizing quadratic functions as distinct from other functions, say cubic functions? (We are still speaking about situations and not the symbolized forms of these situations, of course.) Can we tell one from the other? For example:

'There are as many carriages in a train as the number of compartments in a carriage, *and* as the number of seats in a compartment. When the train starts, every seat is taken and nobody is standing. At the first stop a lot more people want to get on, so that six more carriages are put on, of the same kind as the other carriages. All the seats are exactly taken up in this new portion. At the next station they put on one more carriage in which again all the seats are taken, but this one has eleven compartments though the size of the compartments is still the same. Only six more people want to get on so that it is not worth putting on another carriage. They therefore stand in the corridor. When the train reaches the border, they all have to change because the railways in the next country have a different gauge. In the new country the coaches are bigger, i.e. they have more compartments, and more seats in a compartment. They can just fit all the people in a train so that all the seats are taken and no one is standing.

(a) How many more carriages are there in this train than in the one that started before any carriages were put on?

(b) How many more compartments are there in the new carriages than in the old ones?

(c) How many more people can sit in a compartment in a new carriage than in a compartment in an old carriage?'

This is a cubic problem and embodies the factorization of the cubic function

$$x^3+6x^2+11x+6=(x+1)(x+2)(x+3)$$

so that 'one more', 'two more', and 'three more' are the answers to the questions, but of course in any order.

A 'train' embodiment of a quadratic function problem would be as follows:

'There are as many carriages in a train as the number of compartments in a carriage. These are all filled by the time the train starts, but no one has to stand. They put on six more carriages at the next stop and these get exactly filled up. At the next station they put on an extra carriage with nine compartments and all the seats again get exactly filled up. At the border all the people have to change, because in the new country they have a different gauge. In the new country the carriages are bigger; they have more compartments, but the same number of seats in each compartment as before. They just manage to seat every one with all the seats taken and no one standing.

(a) How many more carriages are there on this train than on the one that started before any carriages were put on?

(b) How many more compartments are there in a carriage in this country than in the old one?'

This is the embodiment of the factorization of the quadratic function

$$x^2+6x+9=(x+3)(x+3)=(x+3)^2$$

therefore three more compartments per carriage and three more carriages on the train are the answers to the problem.

The difference between a quadratic and a cubic function is just that the *variable* in the quadratic occurs up to the second power in the quadratic, but up to the third power in the cubic. The seats per compartment, the compartments per carriage and the carriages per train is the *variable* in the cubic problem, since it can be arbitrarily chosen without affecting the solution of the problem. In the quadratic problem the number of compartments per carriage, this being the same as the number of carriages per train, is the relevant variable. People are transferred in blocks, each block filling a compartment, and so these blocks are really the mathematical units in terms of which the other groups are counted. The detection of the difference between the two types of problems could have been made easier by working with people, compartments and carriages, instead of with compartments, carriages and trains, in which case the units in terms of which the relevant groups are counted would have been more obvious. This would have reduced the train to a Diesel one-carriage affair, with six more compartments in it than seats per compartment and nine people standing, all other seats being occupied.

Of course it can be objected that the second problem, because of the way it is formulated, is a cubic problem, since the number of people per compartment is really a variable. But it is a useless one that does not come into the problem. If y is this number, and the units are the people and not the compartments, the symbolized version of the problem is really

$$x^2y + 6xy + 9y = (x+3)^2y$$

The *problem* still consists in sorting out the x's, since the y occurs as a factor in every term; this problem is still a quadratic one.

To be able to tell one such situation from another is a task of some difficulty. If a child is able to select the quadratic types from a random selection of quadratic, cubic and other types of problems, he is certainly able to identify the exemplars of the quadratic function situations. If he cannot do this, can we really say that he *knows* what quadratic functions are? Can a person who thinks that a table is a chair be said to *know* what tables and chairs are?

To sum up: in relation to a mathematical structure, situations fall into three categories:

(a) situations irrelevant to the structure,

(b) situations relevant to the structure which are exemplars of the class of situations described by the structure,

(c) situations relevant to the structure which are non-exemplars of the class of situations described by the structure.

The distinction between non-exemplars and irrelevancies is to a certain extent arbitrary, and depends on the class of situations which we choose to regard as relevant. For example we might be talking about buying furniture for a new house, in which case the relevant situations would be furniture (i.e. its choosing, buying, making, etc.). We might be out on an expedition on which we were hoping to buy a table. We could walk into a furniture store and see a Jacobean table. This is an exemplar of the class of tables. We might also see displayed some beautiful spindle-backs that would go nicely with the table. These spindle-backs are certainly relevant, but they would be non-exemplars of the kind of thing we were out to acquire that day. We might wander into another department of the store where we see a dress we would like to buy for our little girl. This is quite irrelevant to the buying of furniture for our new house. Logicians call the class of relevant situations the *universe of discourse*. It is the universe of things about which we happen to be discoursing at the moment. Anything which belongs to this universe is relevant at the moment; other things outside it are irrelevant. We then pick out a class of things *within* this universe of discourse. Members of this class will be exemplars of the class picked; other members of the universe of discourse will be non-exemplars. Much of the trouble we meet with in mathematics concerns non-exemplars, as they often do not form a well defined class of things, events or situations. To permit the class of non-exemplars to be well defined, the universe of discourse needs to be well defined.

If children are to grasp relationships rapidly and effectively in relation to any mathematical structure we want them to learn, we must present them with several embodiments of this structure within a certain universe of discourse, followed by embodiments of other structures in the same universe of discourse, to help them to tell the difference between the exemplars and non-exemplars. This involves the use of two principles, which we might formulate as

(a) the principle of *multiple embodiment*,[1] and
(b) the principle of *contrast*.

The presentation of many embodiments will ensure that eventually only the essentially mathematical structure is retained out of all the embodied situations, so that exemplars not previously encountered will nevertheless be recognized as having the mathematical structure in question. The contrast examples are to ensure that situations not possessing the structure will be recognized as not possessing it.

It is a truism that mathematical concepts are constructed out of mathematical variables. *A priori*, for the effective learning of a mathematical concept, all the inherent mathematical variables should be varied in the learner's experience. It would be useless to teach $(x+y)^2=x^2+2xy+y^2$ by restricting the value of y to one or only a few values. How could the relationship be learnt if all that is encountered is $(x+1)^2=x^2+2x+1$? This, of course, is obvious enough. In other areas of mathematics it does not seem to be taken quite so much for granted. For example, the concept of place-value notation is based on (a) a base number; (b) powers of the base number; (c) the number of each power of the base number present. This concept is severely restricted by keeping the base number a constant, namely ten. It is further restricted by the limited variation of the exponent to which the base number is raised to obtain the various powers. The only variable that is copiously varied is the one

[1] In *Building up mathematics* this principle was referred to as the *perceptual variability principle*

listed under (c), the digits of the numbers which are used for children's interminable 'sums'. It is not surprising that, even after endless successions of such 'sums', they have only a hazy idea of the concept of place value.

We have previously referred to the principle of varying all the relevant mathematical concepts as the *mathematical variability principle*. It is by the maximum variation of the variables that we ensure that what is essentially invariant during the variation is seen. If something remains always the same, we tend not to see it. A moving object is noticed more forcibly than one that is at rest. A 'moving' mathematical structure will likewise stand out and be noticed.

Apart from observing the principles of multiple embodiment, of contrast and of mathematical variation, there are many other steps we can take to make the process of learning mathematical structures more effective and more enjoyable for children. A punishment-reward system deflects them from appraising the intrinsic interest of what they are doing and directs them towards the more selfish ends of gaining favour or avoiding disfavour. We could do a great deal for our children's ethical as well as intellectual development by doing away with rewards and punishments, and substituting as intrinsic motivation the interest of the task itself. It is quite surprising how children will take an interest in unravelling abstract structures and their properties without any extrinsic push being necessary.

No more will be said here on the subject of individual work or intrinsic motivation, as this has been discussed in a number of recent publications.[1] Research is in progress in many parts of the world on the conditions necessary to improve the efficiency of mathematics-learning, as well as on the more fundamental problems of how the process of mathematics-learning takes place at all. The work of Piaget is well known,[2] and research in Geneva goes on apace into

[1] *Building up mathematics* Chapter I and *The creative use of mathematics in the Junior School* L. G. W. Sealey

[2] *The child's conception of number* and *Sur la construction du nombre* Piaget, Greco, Grize, 1961

the fundamental questions. During the academic year 1960–1 the Harvard University Center for Cognitive Studies ran a Mathematics-Learning Project, planned and executed by Jerome Bruner and myself, the report on which is now published. Other research has been or is being carried out by Skemp in Manchester, Sealey and Oldridge in Leicestershire, the National Foundation for Educational Research for England and Wales in Surrey and elsewhere, Robert Davis in Syracuse, N.Y., and Suppes in California. Other projects have been started in Florence, Budapest, Adelaide, Hawaii, Minnesota and elsewhere.

2

The Study of Powers, Roots and Logarithms

AS RESEARCH progresses, it becomes increasingly clear that there is very little mathematics that cannot be taught at the secondary stage; even at the primary stage a great deal more could be taught than is taught now. We have been seriously underestimating what children are capable of, provided we create favourable conditions and use appropriate methods. What follows has been found suitable for children between the ages of ten and thirteen.

There are two different ways in which embodiments of mathematical structures can be presented to children. One is to put in their hands material so designed that through controlled manipulation certain mathematical relationships will become clear. During what Piaget has called the concrete operational stage (which coincides approximately with the Junior School years) it is quite essential that concepts new to children should be learnt through their own experiences.[1] As they move into the stage in which they can make hypothetical deductions, it is possible more and more to dispense with actual experience and rely on imagined operations. 'If we did this, so and so would happen' becomes a more possible line of attack with children of twelve or thirteen. Younger children will actually have to see what does happen, and concrete material can enormously accelerate the learning process. However, it must not be thought that concrete materials have no place during the later years of adolescence. They serve to confirm that what

[1] Z. P. Dienes, 'On learning of mathematical concepts by children through experience' *Educational Research*, November, 1959

has been learnt really does happen, much as an experiment in physics or chemistry goes hand in hand with theoretical study. At the same time, relationships can be illuminated by the use and enrichment of the imagery which corresponds to the relationships being learnt. For this reason, two rather different ways of handling the powers, roots and logarithms relationships will be given. One relies on concrete experiences consisting of actual physical handling of material, the other plays on the children's imagination by the use of what may be called the mathematical story.

The concrete material used will have to embody physically the structure of powers. This is not very difficult. We select a base number, for example 2. We also select a unit, in terms of which we shall measure the pieces of material. This for example could be a centimetre cube, i.e. a cube whose edges are one centimetre long. (If inches are preferred, $\frac{3}{8}$ of an inch is quite close to 1 centimetre.) The next piece will be 2 units placed together at one face, making a rectangular box shape. We can stick 2 of these box shapes together, making a flat square shape. 2 of these flat square shapes on top of one another will yield a cube, which will now consist of 8 units. 2 such cubes may be put together to make a larger box shape, 2 such box shapes to make a larger flat square shape, and 2 of these to make a yet larger cube. We have now reached a piece with 64 units in it. This is of course the 6th power of 2. By the time we reach the 12th power we have a cube whose edges are 16 cm. long. It is not actually necessary to build these shapes out of units. They can be cut from timber, the larger pieces being more conveniently made hollow.[1]

Similarly there can be a series of blocks where the number 3 is taken as the base number, but in this case it is only practicable to go as far as the 9th power of 3. Other series to the bases 4 and 5 may be constructed, though these

[1] This material, to bases 2, 3, 4 and 5, known as the Logs and Indices Blocks or LIB, may be obtained, complete with manual for teachers and instruction cards for children, from the National Foundation for Educational Research, 79 Wimpole Street, London W.1

could not go much beyond the 6th power without becoming too unwieldy for classroom use. Naturally the higher the base number, the sooner we shall reach impossible proportions, as the volumes increase in geometrical progression.

If the work is undertaken with juniors or with first-year secondary school children, it is very instructive to pile out the contents of all the boxes on a table and let a group of four to six children sort them out into piles. It is advisable, if this is done, to have as many of each kind of piece as the base-number, i.e. 2 of each piece in base 2, 3 of each piece in base 3 and so on, with the possible exception of the largest piece in each series. If children are asked to sort the blocks into four piles they often sort them into three piles at first by the 'look' of the pieces, i.e. the boxes in one pile, the square-looking shapes in another, and the cubes in another. A hint about how the pieces are related to one another often produces three different piles, a 3-base, a 5-base and a combined 2- and 4-base. This is where a more searching question about how the piles are made up will nearly always produce a separation of the joint pile into a 2-pile and a 4-pile. As soon as the *internal* structure of each pile has been understood, that is, as soon as children begin to say: '3 of those make that, 3 of those make that, and then 3 of those will make that one . . .', the analytical insight has been achieved. The joint pile is seen not to conform to the structure just discovered in the 3-pile and the 5-pile, and so it is taken apart. This is a beautiful example of an almost entirely constructive piece of work leading to the physical construction of a structure, followed by the analysis of what has been constructed. The 'play' at first is quite random, but the instruction about sorting the blocks into piles accelerates the search for regularities in the mass of material on the table. Certain regularities are found, and eventually the 3-pile and the 5-pile are built up with the largest piece at the bottom, working up to the units being placed on top. Once they have discovered the rule-structure, they play the game by the rules and find that one of the piles does not conform. So they take steps to ensure that it does. It is this rule-bound play that finally fixes their analytical insight into the ratio properties of the piles.

It is now time to 'play with', instead of 'playing towards', these ratios. The children can be asked to put one series out in a row, say the 2-series, beginning with the unit and putting a single piece of each size in ascending order of size. The next piece (2 units) is denoted the 1-position, the next one the 2-position, and so on up to the 12-position. Moving up one space along the track, we always come to a piece consisting of 2 times as many units as the one from which we have just moved. Moving up two spaces along the track, we find a piece with 4 times as many units in it as the one we have moved from. This is just the number of units at the 2-position. In general, moving up k steps is a multiplication of the piece from which we move up by exactly as much as the number of units lying at the k-position. Whatever is lying at any position is of course the result of multiplying the unit by as much as the number of units in that position. At the r-position for example we shall find of course 2^r units. If we move up k steps, we multiply by 2^k, and we shall find ourselves at the (r+k) position. So

$$2^k.2^r=2^{k+r}$$

One of the difficulties here, as always when operators and operands are handled, is that 'numbers' are used as counters of the number of units that there are in a piece, and also as multipliers or operators which turn these numbers into other numbers. The number 2^3 may simply refer to the piece consisting of 8 units; it may also indicate a command to find a piece which consists of eight times as many units as a certain piece. The fact that the command and the piece can be inverted is a curious mathematical phenomenon known as the commutative law of multiplication. The piece 2^3 multiplied by 2^4 is 2^7, and it is really rather curious that likewise the piece 2^4 multiplied by 2^3 is 2^7. This is something children should appreciate, possibly through being shown *non*-commutative situations, which abound in daily life. Opening the window and putting one's head out clearly presents a non-commutative pair of events. Similarly when making a sauce, we shall clearly get different results if we put the fat or the flour in the pan first. Even in the field of mathematics it is not hard to think of examples: multiplying by 2 and adding 3 will have different results according to the order in which we perform the operations. This is the *principle of contrast.* Commutativity is only appreciated by the experience of non-commutativity.

Let us now consider how children can proceed from the additive law of indices. The law governing division of powers is easily discovered by taking steps towards the 'start' or zero-position. Each reverse step entails a division by 2; two such steps a division by 4 and so on. If we take r steps backwards from the k-position we shall be at the $(k-r)$ position, provided $k \geqslant r$. At the k-position there is a piece consisting of 2^k units; going back r steps is dividing by 2^r because each of the r steps is a division by 2. So we have

$$2^k/2^r = 2^{k-r}$$

There is a danger that children will learn the rules too soon. If so, they will mechanize the procedure, as they do in the conventional classroom situation. The questions must then be re-formulated so that the rule has to be used intelligently and not mechanically. For example, one might say: 'Here is a piece. Share this piece out into as many equal parts as there are units in that piece over there,' or else, 'Taking as many of these pieces as there are units in that piece over there, which other piece could you make with them exactly?' These are actual, even if schematic, situations. If they are coped with intelligently, then the thread between the rule-structure and its experiential origin has not been broken, and the rule-structure can be fed back into further experience.

In order to observe the mathematical variability principle, it is necessary to make use of the series to the other bases. The four bases 2, 3, 4 and 5 have been found in practice to contain sufficient mathematical variation on which children will base a fairly solid mathematical structure. (A fractional base like $1\frac{1}{2}$ or $2\frac{1}{2}$ might also prove useful, only the pieces would tend to be more muddling for beginners. They could easily be made in two dimensions only, out of cardboard or hardboard. Every piece in the series, as well as the pieces out of which they can be made, should be available.)

Apart from the mathematical variability principle and the contrast principle, how can we observe the multiple embodiment principle? For base 2 it is easy to make a two-dimensional variant of the three-dimensional blocks with successive squares and rectangles only. For base 3 we should start from an equilateral triangle as a unit, perhaps 1 cm. thick, with sides 2 cm. long. Three of these put together in one plane would make an isosceles trapezium and three of the latter would make another equilateral triangle. We have now put together 27, i.e. 3^3 unit triangles. Suppose we take three such triangles and place them on top of one another. We shall get a thicker triangle: its thickness will be 3 cm. We shall now have 81 unit triangles. We can put these together again in threes, making larger (and thicker) trapezia, which will now have 243 unit triangles in them. We can put these together in threes and make further equilateral triangles; we can then make these thicker by putting three together in layers and go on until the limits of practicality are reached. The 12th power would be an equilateral triangle 27 cm. thick and 54 cm. long along each side. This would be somewhat unwieldy, so it is better to stop at the 8th power, which is 18 cm. long and 9 cm. thick. The base 4 can be embodied also in triangular shapes, but without any intervening trapezia, since four triangles can be built into another similar triangle. Then four such triangles can be placed together in layers, four of these bigger triangles put together to make a similar but larger triangle, and so on. To avoid the 'triangles' becoming tall triangular prisms, it is advisable here to start with a unit triangle $\frac{1}{2}$ cm.

thick, whose sides are 2 cm. long. Even then, by the 6th power the prism will be 32 cm. tall, whereas the length of an edge of a cross-section parallel to the base would be only 16 cm. An alternative way would be to make the 2nd power of 4 by putting 16 unit triangles in one plane, making a triangle out of them. The 3rd power could be obtained by putting four of these in layers, and so on; not a great deal is gained by this procedure, as naturally the final volume of the piece representing 4^6 unit triangles will be the same, however constructed.

It is not strictly necessary to go to such lengths to observe the principle of multiple embodiment. The ratio-relationships can be expressed conventionally. One might use the colours of the rainbow, with each colour 'worth' the base number times the previous colour. The colours could be counters or pegs or even cards. The same exercises could be carried out with these pegs or cards as were carried out with the rectangular blocks. Or imaginary situations can be thought out that have the same structure. Someone might be breeding guinea pigs. He starts with a guinea pig which gives birth to one male and two females. The two females in turn each give birth to a male and two females, and so it goes on for twelve generations. All the females, after they have given birth to their babies, are put in cages, while the males are sold. Every generation is kept in a separate section. Section 1 is the original two female babies which were born first. Section 2 is the second generation, and so on, until we have reached section 12, which is the twelfth generation. Similar exercises could now be carried out on the various generations of guinea pigs as were carried out with the blocks. Or if dying a heroic death is preferred to giving birth, battles can take place in which always the same proportion of the whole army perish. Suppose that $\frac{2}{3}$ of the army perishes in the first battle, $\frac{2}{3}$ of the remaining army in the second battle, etc., until after nine battles there is just one soldier left. Whether he should die a heroic death can be left to the children. The army must be given rations in between battles, say each soldier gets a pint of beer and a tin of bully beef. Questions can now be put about the way the problems of the field kitchen change from one lull to another in the fighting, depending on the numbers to be catered for.

Raising powers to other powers can be done on the tracks very easily, and so can the extraction of roots. For example: 'Look at this piece. Find out how many units it has in it. Imagine just as many of these pieces as this number; which other piece could you make with them exactly?' This is a squaring problem, and not many exercises are necessary before children realize that such problems are solved by doubling the position numbers. A square root problem may be presented as follows: 'Look at this piece, call it piece A. Now look towards the zero position, choose another piece, and call this piece B. How many pieces B do you need to have to make piece A? How many units are there in piece B? *Are these two numbers the same?* If they are not, go on looking for a piece B which has exactly as many units in it as there are pieces B in piece A.' The number of units in piece B is the square root of the number of units in piece A. A cubing problem could be put as follows: 'Look at this piece, call it piece X. Find the piece which has as many pieces X in it as the piece X has units in it. Call this piece Y. Then find the piece which has as many pieces Y in it as X has units in it. Call this piece Z.' Piece Z embodies the cube of piece X. That the cubing involves a trebling of the position number, the cube-rooting on the other hand its division by 3, will quite quickly be discovered by the children. Once again we must vary the bases and the exponents as much as possible. It may also be necessary to check on the degree of abstraction achieved by supplying either different material or imagined situations in which the children should know how to apply the structure they have learnt.

The multiplying and dividing of the position numbers, i.e. of the exponents, may have been linked with raising to a power or extracting a root, without fractional exponents being thought of, because the association has been with the operation and not with the number in question each time.

To introduce fractional exponents, we need to get the children to work on larger bases. For example a series of cubes might be put out, representing a track on the base 8:

Number of units in piece	1	8	64	512	4096	etc.
Position number of piece	0	1	2	3	4	etc.

Suppose we now give the problem of finding the cube root of 64. If the children have learnt the rule of taking one-third of the position number to discover the piece which is the cube root of 64, then they will be looking for a piece $\frac{1}{3}$ of the way from the zero-position to the 2-position. In fact there ought to be a $\frac{2}{3}$-position. In the 2-series there are two pieces in between the 1 and the 8, they are the 2 and the 4. So it is the 4 which should be at the $\frac{2}{3}$-position in the 8-series. Similarly, 2 being the cube root of 8, it should be $\frac{1}{3}$ of the way up from the zero-position to the 1-position, so 2 should be at the $\frac{1}{3}$-position. Then the rest of the series may be filled in with pieces and the corresponding position-numbers. The 4-series and the 9-series can be constructed, and filled in with fractional position-numbers whose denominators are 2. The base 64 is an interesting base to take, as the intervening position-numbers will have denominators 2, 3 and 6.

This work is somewhat risky, as children will readily grasp the formal structure of what is happening, but may lose the thread connecting it with the number-relationships which the structure expresses. If the exponent notation has been introduced, one might ask what $8^{\frac{2}{3}}$ is. The answer might be immediate and correct, namely 4; but this may only be the application of the 'rule', that you have to find two-thirds of the position-number of 8, i.e. $\frac{2}{3}$ of 1. The more testing question, 'If you are allowed to take roots and raise to powers, and you are allowed to do each of these once only, how can you reach 4 if you start from 8?' might be greeted with complete blankness. Even if it is worked out that you can take the cube root and obtain 2, then square and so obtain 4, or that you can at first square 8 and obtain 64, of which the cube root is 4, it is not at all certain that the cube-rooting will be associated with the 3 in the denominator of $\frac{2}{3}$, or the squaring with the 2 in the numerator. Once, however, this connexion is made between what really is happening and the formal procedure of 'going $\frac{2}{3}$ of the way', etc., then the fractional exponent is beginning to acquire a safe position in the learnt rule-structure.

The eventual result of 'playing with' the rule-structure of the properties of ratios has been a deep analysis of the relationships between powers and roots. The first random game with the blocks, i.e. sorting them out, was a 'playing *towards*' the construction of the ratio properties of the blocks. The subsequent activity was a 'playing *with*' these properties, in a game whose rule-structure was beginning to become familiar through use. Playing the game of ratios by the gradually emerging rules resulted in an analysis of the roots-and-powers situation. It may still be possible to deepen this analysis by further rule-bound play. If, for example, it is not certain whether the inverse properties of powers and roots have been fully appreciated, certain 'games' could be played with that insight in view. The more these and other games are played, the more the properties of the blocks will tend to become the playthings, rather than the blocks themselves. The blocks have changed their significance, and are now acting as symbols for the number of units contained in them—much as the symbols x^n, etc., will act as symbols for a certain number of units. This process will be gone into more fully in later chapters.

If the structure of powers and roots, with the accompanying symbolism, has been grasped, logarithms will present no problem. A logarithm is only another name for an exponent. If we explain that in any series the logarithm of the number of units in a block is the position-number of that block, all that has been learnt already can be transferred to logarithms. For example, let us take a piece A and a piece B, multiply the number of units in A by the number of units in B, and call the resulting piece C. The position-number of C will by now be known to be the sum of the position-numbers of A and B. So if we denote by A, B and C the numbers of *units* in these pieces we know that

$$A \times B = C$$

and also that $\log A + \log B = \log C$

When children who have been through the exercises on powers and roots are presented with problems on logarithms in this way, they wonder what all the fuss is about; they seem to have learnt it all before. The difficulties that arise in a conventional class spring from not having learnt the powers and roots satisfactorily.

To round off the study of these relationships, it is useful to give children problems in which alternately two of the three items, (a) the base number, (b) the exponent, (c) the whole power, are given and the third one needs to be calculated. For example, we might say, 'In which series is the block with 64 units in it at position-number 3?' The symbolized form of this problem is

$$x^3 = 64$$

where x is to be found. It is of course the 4-series. The answer, 4, is both the number of the series and the number of units at the 1-position. Here, the exponent and the whole power are given, and the base is to be found; the problem is solved by extracting a root.

Again, we might ask, 'How many units are in the piece at the 7-position in series 2?' The answer is 128, and the operation required to find this number is raising 2 to the 7th power. Here, the base number and the exponent are given and the power is to be found. Finally, the problem 'At which position in series 3 is the piece with 81 units in it?' is one of finding the exponent when the base-number and the whole power are given. The answer is 4, which is the logarithm of 81 to the base 3.

This kind of 'rounding-off' will give children a general view of the circle of concepts within which they have been moving, making them confident that the ground is familiar. The more confident they become, the more likely they will be to start manipulating the situation for themselves. In this way we give children a chance to acquire the kind of mathematical daring of which we spoke in the last chapter.

Let us now consider how the same concepts may be covered without the use of any concrete material. We might begin by telling the following story:

A magician lives in a round palace in the middle of a town which he entirely controls. By his magic powers he provides all the money that he thinks the people ought to have. They live in houses along avenues which radiate outwards from the round palace. People living in the same house are always provided with exactly the same allowance of money, so that they can have the same living standard and not be jealous of each other. Along the right-hand sides of the avenues (as seen from the palace, of course) there are houses; there are annexes belonging to the houses along the left-hand sides; the avenues are numbered, as in New York, 1st Avenue, 2nd Avenue, 3rd Avenue, and so on, the avenue numbers increasing counter-clockwise from the 1st Avenue. Rich people live on one side of the town—their avenues occupy only half the town, i.e. they radiate from only one half of the palace. On the other side of the town the poorer people also live along avenues; these are numbered by the same numbers, the avenues being continuations of the 2nd, 3rd and other avenues from the other side of the palace. There is of course also a 1st Avenue in the poor section, a continuation of the 1st Avenue in the rich section.

On each avenue the people in the house nearest to the palace get a daily ration of £1. Their houses are all marked on the door with the numeral zero, i.e. 0. These houses form a circle round the palace. The other houses are numbered 1, 2, 3, 4, . . . etc., as they get further away from the palace. All the other people in the houses in 1st Avenue, whether in the rich or the poor section, also get the same daily ration of £1. But in 2nd Avenue, in the rich section as one walks away from the palace, the occupants of each house get exactly twice as much as the occupants of the previous house. So someone living in house No. 4 will get twice as much as someone living in house No. 3. In 3rd Avenue in the rich section the houses are still numbered 1, 2, 3, 4, . . . etc., as one moves away from the palace, but this time each occupant of a house gets three times as much as an occupant of the previous house. In 4th Avenue, occupants of houses get four times as much as the occupants of the previous house, and so on for all the avenues.

In the poor section the houses are numbered with negative numbers. The house next to the zero-house has the number −1 on it in every avenue, the next house is always −2, and so on. In 2nd Avenue, in the poor section, as one goes away from the palace, occupants of houses get one-half of what the occupants of the previous house get, in 3rd Avenue one-third, and so on.

All the people have their allotted work to do, and the magician's eyes are everywhere all the time, so that he knows whether anyone has done a good day's work or not. Good work is rewarded, bad work is punished. He has a radio system so that he can communicate with any person in his home as soon as he has returned from work. He simply has to utter the magic words and the reward or punishment instantly happens. This always takes the form of an alteration in the daily ration of money. For example:

Hocus 1 in 2nd Avenue means	doubling the ration
Hocus 2 in 2nd Avenue means	quadrupling the ration
Hocus 3 in 2nd Avenue means	multiplying the ration by 8
Hocus 4 in 2nd Avenue means	multiplying the ration by 16.

On the other hand:

Pocus 1 in 2nd Avenue means	halving the ration
Pocus 2 in 2nd Avenue means	quartering the ration

and so on.

According to the rules of the town, anyone who has been

'hocussed' or 'pocussed' has to move to another house in the avenue where people are getting the same money ration.

It will soon become clear that in the rich section 'hocus x' means that you go x houses away from the palace, whereas 'pocus x' means that you move x houses towards the palace. Therefore hocussing is a reward, and pocussing is a punishment.

In the poor section, on the other hand, a 'hocus' involves moving towards the palace; and a 'pocus' takes the recipient further from the palace. (These are counterparts in the story of very important mathematical relationships, and as the children work through the story they must become aware of these relationships, first as properties of the story and later as pure mathematical relationships.)

Incidentally, even for someone in the rich section, a heavy 'pocus' punishment might land him in the poor section. If you live in the house in 3rd Avenue where you get £81 (which is house No. 4), and you are told 'pocus 5', you must divide your ration by 3^5 pounds which means you are landed with £$\frac{1}{3}$ = 6s. 8d. for your ration. Coming down from £81 daily to 6s. 8d. daily means that you come down from house No. 4 to house No. (−1), which is 5 moves down. It must be made clear that going round the circle of zero-houses does not count as a step down because, whether you are in the rich or the poor section, on the zero-circle you are getting only £1 a day ration.

Abraca 1 means	stay where you are
Dabra 1 also means	stay where you are.

This is what people get who have done an average day's work, not too badly but not too well. On the other hand:

Abraca 2 means	your pay is multiplied by the number of pounds you already get daily.
Dabra 2 means	your pay is divided by the number of pounds which multiplied by itself would give your present pay.

For example, if you were getting £25 in 5th Avenue, and you heard the magic words 'abraca 2', your pay would be multiplied by 25 since this is the number of pounds you are getting already, so your new pay would be £625. You were in house No. 2, but now you must move up to house No. 4 in the same avenue. It does not take long to learn that the result is always the doubling of the house-number, even on the poor side. For example, you might be getting 2s. 6d. in 2nd Avenue, i.e. £$\frac{1}{8}$. You heard the magic abraca 2, which is not such good news to you as it was to your friend in 5th Avenue, because this eighth of a pound has now to be multiplied by the number of pounds that you are getting, which is $\frac{1}{8}$. So the magician transports you to a house where you will be earning $\frac{1}{64}$ of a pound, i.e. $3\frac{3}{4}$d. You have moved from house No. (-3) to house No. (-6) and -6 is still the double of -3, so that the magic abraca 2 has still had the effect of doubling the house-number.

A 'dabra 2', on the other hand, results in halving the house-number. In the same way, just as abraca 2 and dabra 2 are the fictional equivalents of squaring and taking the square root, so abraca 3 and dabra 3 are the equivalents of cubing and taking the cube root.

Abraca 3 means	your pay is multiplied by the number of pounds you are getting already; and then this amount is again multiplied by the number of pounds you are getting already.
Dabra 3 means	you must go to the house from which an abraca 3 would have brought you to your present house.

This formulation does, of course, 'give away' the inverse property. If this is not desired, a more 'first principle' explanation of dabra 3 can be given.

The magician one day decides to play a game with himself and to give out all the punishments and rewards without uttering 'hocus-pocus', only 'abraca-dabra'. He allows himself to give each person two successful magic commands. He might want to bring down a person in 4th Avenue who is getting £256 to a mere £64. He could do it by a pocus 1, but can he do it with abraca-dabras? He can administer a dabra 4, followed by an abraca 3. This brings his victim down to £4, then brings him up to £64. This can be followed by more ambitious commands, the results of which might be a move to another avenue. For example a dabra 3 administered to a person in 8th Avenue getting £64 ought to be £4, because his house-number is No. 2 which has to be divided by 3, giving a house-number $\frac{2}{3}$. To complete the avenue

1, 8, 64, 512, . . . etc.

to include thirds and two-thirds, we should have to have

1, 2, 4, 8, 16, 32, 64, 128, 256, 512, . . . in our avenue.

In the absence of houses in 8th Avenue where such amounts are being earned, our victim would have to move either to house No. 1 in 4th Avenue or to house No. 2 in 2nd Avenue. The magician one day decides to dispense with all this moving from avenue to avenue, and has houses built all along the avenues at all points to which it would be possible to magic people. These new houses naturally acquire fractional numbers. It should be clear now how the cover story will help to introduce all the necessary concepts surrounding integral, fractional, positive and negative exponents. The house-numbers are the logarithms of the amounts people are getting, to the base which is the number of the avenue. The base-number (i.e. the pay in house No. 1) is the n-th root of the pay in the n-th house in any avenue, as a dabra n will land someone from house No. n into house No. 1. The power is the amount of pay in each house, where the avenue-number is raised to the power which is indicated by the house-number.

It could make interesting home-work to ask children to make up further stories to embody the structure learnt. Even if they cannot represent all of it in an original story, they might be able to manage some of it, and so gradually they can learn the feel and the power of the structure they have been in contact with. We shall come back in a later chapter to the fundamental considerations concerning underlying mathematical imagery.

We have extended integral exponents to fractional exponents through natural extensions of circumstances. We can likewise extend integral bases to fractional bases. It has already been suggested, at one stage, that material to the base $1\frac{1}{2}$ and $2\frac{1}{2}$ should be constructed. This can be extended to other fractions, and also introduced into the cover story. Why not have a $1\frac{1}{2}$ Avenue? Or a $2\frac{1}{2}$ Avenue? Or a $1\frac{1}{3}$ Avenue? What would people get in house No. 1 in $2\frac{1}{2}$ Avenue? What about house No. 2? The squares of numbers such as $2\frac{1}{2}$ are best worked out on squared paper, by the actual drawing of two and a half rows of two and a half squares. It is quite extraordinary how many children reach the ages of eleven to thirteen without having the least comprehension of the *real* properties of fractions of *real* things, even if they have learnt a number of formal rules. They simply see no connexion between the formal rules learnt and the corresponding situations in reality. For this reason, in what follows we shall base all the exercises involving fractions on 'first principles'.

Returning to our imaginary town, suppose that we are now able to have as many avenues as we like in between the existing 'whole number' avenues. The magician might choose to set up a $1\frac{1}{120}$ Avenue. In house No. 0 they will still be getting £1. In house No. 1 they will be getting £1. 0s. 2d. But what will they be getting in house No. 2? It will be

$$\pounds(1+\tfrac{1}{120})(1+\tfrac{1}{120})$$

This can be worked out on squared paper or graph paper, representing a pound by a square 120 by 120. The one-hundred-and-twentieth of a pound can be represented by a thin strip 1 by 120, which we can join on to the square representing the £1. We need to take this $1\frac{1}{120}$ times, which results in something like the following diagram.

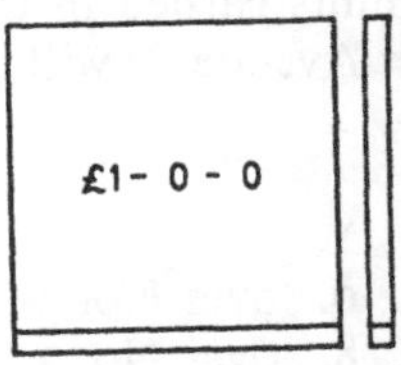

The part of the figure on the left is

$$(1+\tfrac{1}{120})$$

and the part of the figure on the right is

$$\tfrac{1}{120}\text{th of } (1+\tfrac{1}{120})$$

It is clear that occupants of house No. 2 will be earning

$$£\left(1+\tfrac{2}{120}+\tfrac{1}{120}\times\tfrac{1}{120}\right)$$

Supposing now that the magician invents another kind of magic. He decides to call it differus. It goes like this:

Differus $\frac{1}{2}$ means that wherever you are, you move up half an avenue—i.e. if you are on 4th Avenue, you move to $4\frac{1}{2}$ Avenue, or if you are on $2\frac{1}{2}$ Avenue, you move up to 3rd Avenue—but you keep the same house-number. You do not go and live there, only find out *how much more* the people in that house are earning than yourself. You then take *two times the difference* and this will be your *rise* in pay. With what you have been earning before, *plus* this rise, you move into annex $\frac{1}{2}$ across the avenue from where you have been living.

Differus $\frac{1}{4}$ would mean moving up one-quarter of an avenue, i.e. to $1\frac{1}{4}$ Avenue and visiting the house of the same number as your own. Here you would again find out the difference between what you are earning and what they are earning. Multiply this difference by 4, and this would be your rise in pay over and above what you were getting already. You would move into annex $\frac{1}{4}$ across the avenue. (The multiplying by 4 is really the same as dividing by a quarter.)

Differus h would mean moving up h units of avenue-change and finding out how much more than you they are earning in that avenue in the house with the same house-number as yourself. You would divide this number by h to give your rise, and with your new pay move into annex No. h.

It is instructive to work out the amounts earned in the annexes across the way from No. 2 in 1st Avenue. It will be found that

		£	s.	d.	
annex No. $\frac{1}{2}$	has a rise	2.	10.	0.	over No. 2
annex No. $\frac{1}{3}$	has a rise	2.	6.	8.	over No. 2

		£	s.	d.	
annex No. $\frac{1}{4}$	has a rise	2.	5.	0.	over No. 2
annex No. $\frac{1}{8}$	has a rise	2.	2.	6.	over No. 2
annex No. $\frac{1}{10}$	has a rise	2.	2.	0.	over No. 2
annex No. $\frac{1}{120}$	has a rise	2.	0.	2.	over No. 2
annex No. $\frac{1}{480}$	has a rise	2.	0.	$0\frac{1}{2}$.	over No. 2

It will soon be apparent that, whenever you get a differus instruction from house No. 2 in 1st Avenue, your rise is bound to be more than £2. 0s. 0d. People going to annex No. h will be getting the same pay as people on (1+h) Avenue in house No. 1 *plus* £2. 0s. 0d. The circle of No. 2 houses represents the function x^2, and the amount of rise which a differus magic is certain to entail at each avenue is the differential coefficient of x^2 for the value of x which is the avenue number. These should be tabulated for all the avenues, as follows

Avenue-number	1	2	3	4	5	6	7	8	9	. . . →
Amount of certain rise	2	4	6	8	10	12	14	16	18	. . . →

It is then possible to introduce a zero-annex, where that amount of rise is given which any differus magic would have given, whatever fraction or number might have accompanied it.

The values found for the amount *more* earned in the zero-annexes than in the 'parent' houses represent the differential coefficient of the function which connects the base-houses with the 'parent' houses. The base-houses are of course the houses No. 1, and the amount earned in these houses is the number of the base which is raised to successive powers as we move along the avenues away from the palace. The relationship between the base-houses, the 'parent' houses and the corresponding zero-annexes will be clearer if the values of both the functions are tabulated together:

Number of £ earned in base-house	x	1	2	3	4	5	6	7	8	9
Number of £ earned in house No. 2	x^2	1	4	9	16	25	36	49	64	81
Number of pounds *more* earned in zero-annex to No. 2 than in No. 2	$2x$	2	4	6	8	10	12	14	16	18

If the number of £ earned in the base-house is x, the amount earned in No. 2 is x^2, where x is the number of the avenue. The amount more that the occupants of the zero-annexes have, compared with the corresponding houses across the avenues, is always 2x, i.e. twice as much as the number of £ earned in the base-house in that avenue. In mathematical language, we say that 2x is the differential coefficient of the function x^2. In this way the limiting process underlying the notion is built into the construction, and there can be no nonsense about 'dividing zero by zero'. All the annexes are, however, necessary before the problem of the zero-annex can be tackled.

There is no royal road to the calculus, but the imagery generated by such a story is nevertheless a great help. It does not skip the mathematical difficulties, but faces them fairly and squarely as they occur. Strangely enough, children seem to enjoy and appreciate this.

Naturally, finding the differential coefficient of one function, namely of x^2, is by no means enough to get the feel of the sort of thing that can happen in this new field of mathematics. It might be objected that the functions x^3, x^4, . . . are too complex, that children in their early teens would not be able to cope with the intricacies involved in computing their differential coefficients. The binomial expansions to the respective powers are involved, and this might be thought to put it out of younger children's reach. But teachers need not be daunted. Once children have learnt to enjoy the challenge presented by a complex mathematical structure, they will attack problems presented by new structures with alacrity. This needs to be seen to be believed, but teachers who have tried it out know that it is so.

Let us examine for a moment the mathematical structure that is involved in the differential coefficients of the functions $x, x^2, x^3, x^4, \ldots$ etc. The essentially new idea introduced is the idea of limit. We are dealing with a process with the following properties:

(1) There must exist a number which, even if never reached by the members of the set of numbers churned out by the process, can be approximated as closely as desired by choosing suitable members of the set.

(2) There should be only one such number corresponding to the process.

In the examples from the magician's town dealing with moving into the annexes, the limiting value is never reached, nor is the possibility of two limiting numbers touched upon. Most mathematical processes that children will come across when dealing with limit processes are of this kind: the number approximated to is unique; and it is never reached, however far you proceed with the process. (The further refinements of a non-unique limiting number, and of the limiting numbers themselves, being produced by the process, can well be left until later.) Real-life situations of limits can be given by getting children to consider impossible commands such as:

'Come and see me at the last possible moment before 12 o'clock' or 'Go as near as possible to the wall without touching it'.

However near to 12 o'clock we go to see someone, if it is before 12 we could have seen him later. However near we go to the wall, as long as we are not yet there we can go nearer. This is the curious property of a continuous variation of a variable, that whereas in a discrete variation there is always a next value, in continuous variation there is no next or immediately preceding. There is no next moment to the present or to any other moment, nor is there an immediately preceding moment. These are important mathematical insights without which the study of continuous variation involved in the calculus is impossible.

The other important ingredient for the computation of the differential coefficients of the powers of a variable is the binomial expansion. This is far less difficult than might be imagined. One might begin with a pictorial representation of the powers of the variable. One might also start with the powers of $(x+1)$, rather than of the more general $(x+y)$ where both terms in the binome are varied. Assuming that the classical figure for $(x+1)$ lots of $(x+1)$ is already familiar *and* thoroughly understood as the joining of x lots of $(x+1)$ to yet another $(x+1)$, it would be possible to set up $(x+1)$ lots of $(x+1)(x+1)$'s as follows:

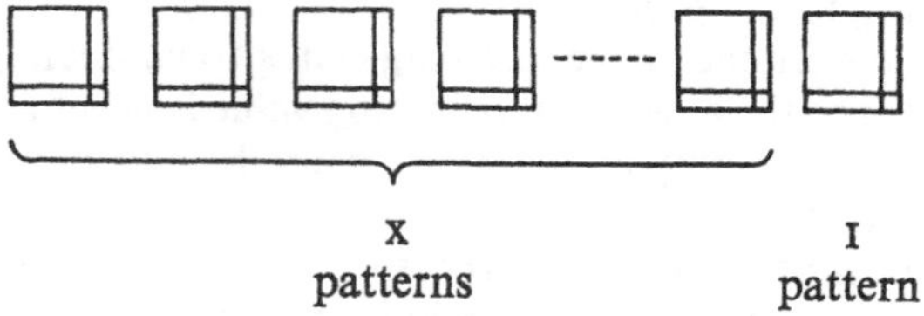

Each pattern contains $(x+1)(x+1)$ units: the large square in each pattern containing x^2 units, the strips x units each, and the small square in each corner being 1 unit. *If the concept of powers is well established*, the following reorganization of the pattern should not cause any difficulties:

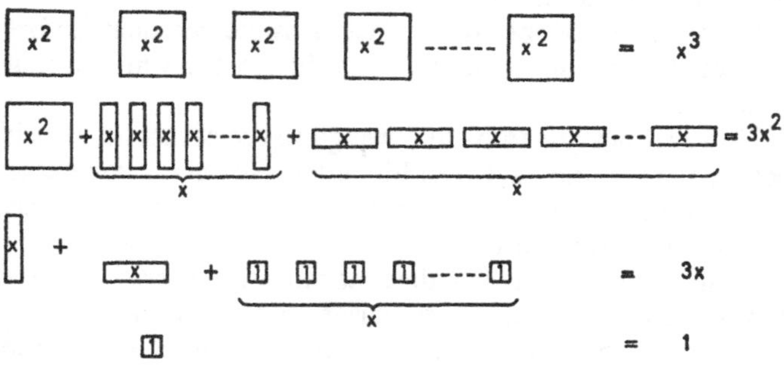

and the binomial expansion of $(x+1)^3 = x^3 + 3x^2 + 3x + 1$ has been attacked by a first experience.

When doing these exercises it is important for children to realize *in practice* that the x lots of units do in fact make a strip, and that x strips do in fact fit together and make a square x by x for any value of x. Pieces of cardboard can be used to make the pieces shown, with as much variation in the value of x as possible. At least three values are suggested as a minimum. This takes care of the necessity of mathematical variation.

It may be desirable to introduce other embodiments, for example three-dimensional embodiments. The LIB referred to earlier (page 44) or the Multi-base Arithmetic Blocks will provide such variation. Alternatively, putting objects in groups, in groups of groups, and in groups of groups of groups, will provide another embodiment, although it is more difficult to disentangle the mathematical structure from the less geometrical embodiments. However, since the geometry of the square and the rectangle are really quite irrelevant to the binomial expansion, it may be found necessary to introduce such non-geometrical equivalents of the geometrical experience. This will be particularly necessary if the children have not learnt the structure *in abstracto* but keep connecting it to squares and rectangles. This state of affairs will be apparent if children cannot *use* the learnt structure in situations in which they have not been taught to use it.

Procedure similar to the one adopted above may be adopted for the study of $(x+1)^4$. In fact $(x+1)^4$ yields a very satisfying repetition of the previous $(x+1)^2$ pattern, by constructing a pattern of the patterns which is of the same structure as the original pattern. (See diagram at top of page 66.)

This arrangement can again be rearranged in descending powers of the variable x. It must be realized that x lots of x^2 units is the same as x^2 lots of x units, both being x^3 units; and that x^2 lots of x^2 units are $x.x.x.x = x^4$ units.

The following rearrangement will not be too difficult for

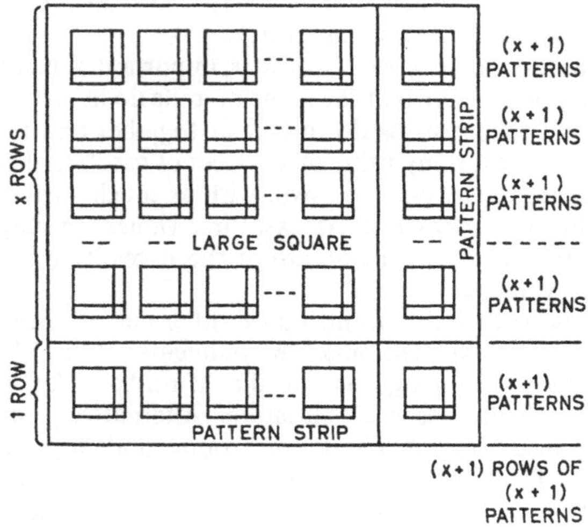

children to discover. It has in fact been successfully achieved by children from secondary modern schools. (See opposite page.)

There will be one x^4. There will be 4 ways in which an x^3 may be collected, in two ways from the pattern-strips and in two ways from the large square. There will be six ways in which an x^2 can be collected, once from the large square, four times out of the small strips in the pattern-strips, and once as the odd square in the bottom right corner of the whole pattern. This leaves two more small x-strips from this same corner and two further lots of singles in two lots of x units from the pattern-strips, making 4x in all. Finally there is the odd unit in the corner of the corner. So altogether

$$(x+1)^4 = x^4 + 4x^3 + 6x^2 + 4x + 1$$

These exercises can be followed up by exercises on the powers of $(x+y)$ where y is at first a whole number. The collecting of the terms takes place in the same way. The small strips will represent xy, and the small square y^2. In

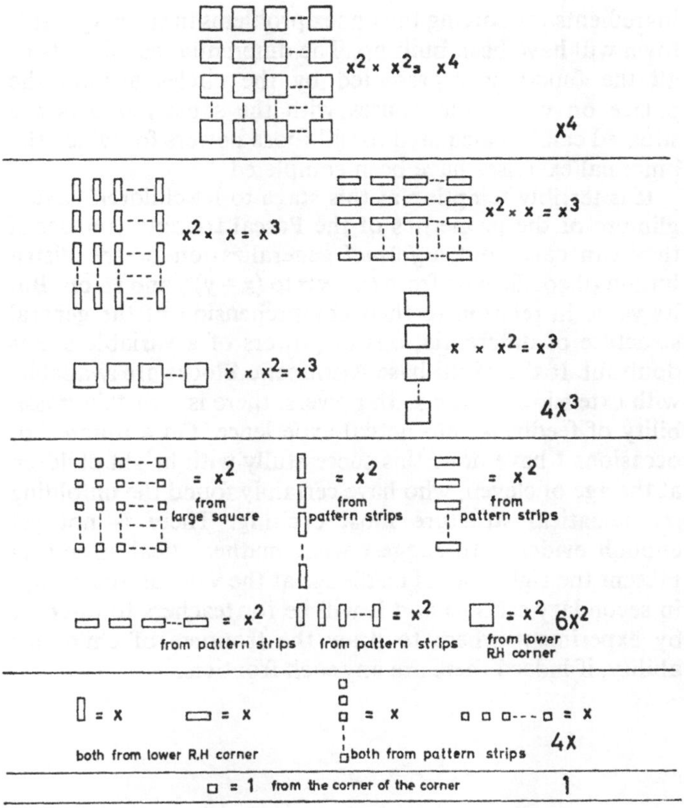

the whole pattern, instead of there being only one column and one row of extra patterns, there will be y rows and y columns. So the number of big squares in a pattern strip will be y times x^3 instead of x^3, the small strips in a pattern-strip will amount to x times xy taken y times, and so on. The sorting out of the powers in descending order, now more than ever, requires a true insight into the properties of powers, including the commutative and associative properties of multiplication. Whole values for y could be followed by fractional values, after which the necessary ingredients for solving the annex problems in the magician's town will have been built up. The differential coefficients of all the functions represented by the circles around the palace on which the houses with the same numbers are situated can be calculated for all those powers for which the binomial exercises have been completed.

It is terribly tempting at this stage to let children have a glimpse of the properties of the Pascal triangle, and see if they can carry out a *formal* generalization of the distribution of coefficients from $(x+y)^4$ to $(x+y)^5$, and so on. But its value in relation to their comprehension of the general structure of differentiations of powers of a variable seems doubtful. If the Multi-base Arithmetic Blocks are available, with extensions to the sixth powers, there is a certain possibility of feedback into actual experience. On a number of occasions I have done this successfully with bright children at the age of eleven, who have certainly found the unfolding mathematical structure most exciting. There is not yet enough evidence to suggest what mathematical structures present the right sort of challenge at the various age-groups in secondary schools and it will be for teachers to discover by experiment where to draw the frontiers of children's ability, if indeed there are any such frontiers.

3

The Mathematical Game

IN THE last chapter we illustrated the functioning of entire cycles of mathematical thinking. We shall now be mostly concerned with one part of the cycle only; that is, the part in which we play the game by the rules. We have encountered this activity as an organic part of a learning cycle, but there is another more artificial type of play.

Anyone who is familiar with a mathematical structure can invent a game whose rules follow the rules of that structure. These can be explained to children, like the rules of any other game, and the game can then be played. This procedure of providing the rules ready made, instead of allowing them to be discovered, starts the learning in rather a closed situation. It need not, however, remain closed. The children can be encouraged to invent games with the same or slightly altered rules. Immediately a new game is being played, the game is one of inventing other games, which is playing a game *about the rules*. When we play a game by its rules, they tell us what we may or may not do with certain things. The situation is closed by the rules. When we are manipulating the rules, instead of the things, the rules themselves have become our playthings. This new 'game' is not really a game yet (although it is certainly play) because we are not aware of the rules that may govern the transformation of rules. It is thus an open situation.

Formally brought-up children will feel insecure in such an exposed position and will ask for more exact guidance. They will be much happier in a closed situation where everything is circumscribed and they merely have to obey the rules. It is for the gradual 'breaking in' (or 'breaking out') of such children that the more severely structured mathematical game will be most useful.

The mathematical ideas whose rule-structures will be translated into mathematical games in this chapter come from the theory of groups and vector spaces. The games described have been successfully played and enjoyed by children between the ages of nine and twelve. Mathematical groups are encountered by children almost as soon as they learn to move about space in a purposive way, and again as soon as they learn about number-operations which can be inverted. In the same way, vector spaces of any number of dimensions are constantly with us; every time we describe a state of affairs quantitatively, we are expressing this as a vector, which has as many dimensions as the number of variables we choose to regard as necessary.

Let us start by giving a few examples of mathematical groups, and go on to extract the properties that a group must have. We shall then be in a position to construct games which will also have these properties.

First example: Displacements in space

Let us assume that we have some way of identifying points in space. Suppose that we are at a point A and then displace ourselves and move to a point B. We can move straight to B by the shortest route, or go a roundabout way, as long as we start at A and finish at B. This displacement we shall call AB. We now move from the point B to the point C, again as we please. This is the displacement BC. We could have moved direct from A to C, by the displacement AC. We can say that the displacement AB followed by BC has the same effect as the displacement AC. We can write

$$AB.BC = AC$$

If we go from A to B, it is also possible to return from B to A. This has the same effect as going from A to A, i.e.

of not going anywhere at all. We shall denote the displacement AA by the figure 1. So

$$AA=1$$

If we do a displacement AB, the displacement which gets us back to where we started from is going to be called the inverse of AB. According to this BA is the inverse of AB. We shall denote this by

$$BA=AB^{-1}$$

Any displacement, followed by its inverse, is equivalent to the displacement 1, which we shall call the unit displacement. So if X is any displacement, we have

$$X.X^{-1}=1$$

It is also obvious that the inverse of the inverse is the original displacement, so that

$$(X^{-1})^{-1}=X$$

If we go from A to B, then from B to C, then from C to D, we have gone from A to D. We could have replaced the first two displacements by AC, or the last two by BD, and we should in either case still have finished at D. So that

$$AC.CD=AB.BD=AD \quad \text{or more fully written out}$$
$$(AB.BC).CD=AB.(BC.CD)=AD$$

In this example we are dealing with displacements, which are the 'things' we are talking about. All we have done is to combine two of them and thereby obtain a third one.

Second example

Let us take fractions as our 'things'. We can restrict ourselves to positive fractions, but must include in the term 'fraction' all whole positive numbers as well as fractions greater than 1. We know that

(i) If we take any two fractions and multiply them, we obtain another fraction;

(ii) If we multiply any number by a fraction p/q, and then multiply the resulting fraction by q/p, we shall obtain the number that we started with, i.e. it is as though we had multiplied by 1.

Thus, a multiplication by q/p is the inverse of the multiplication by p/q. We can write

$$q/p=(p/q)^{-1}$$

Again, if x and y are fractions so that one is the inverse of the other,

$y=x^{-1}$ and $x=y^{-1}$ and $x.y=1$ and so $x.x^{-1}=1$ also $y.y^{-1}=1$

(iii) If we have three fractions x, y and z, it is evident that (x.y) multiplied by z is the same as x multiplied by (y.z), i.e. $(x.y).z=x.(y.z)$.

Exercise for reader. Suppose we have three 'things' and call them α, β and γ. Suppose, also, we agree that we have a 'multiplication' of these things according to the following rules:

$$\begin{array}{lll} \alpha\alpha=\alpha & \alpha\beta=\beta & \alpha\gamma=\gamma \\ \beta\alpha=\beta & \beta\beta=\gamma & \beta\gamma=\alpha \\ \gamma\alpha=\gamma & \gamma\beta=\alpha & \gamma\gamma=\beta \end{array}$$

Is there a 1 in this multiplication? Has every 'thing' got another 'thing' with which, if you multiply it, you get this 1? If so, then every 'thing' has an inverse. Is it always true that

$$(x.y).z=x.(y.z)$$

whatever 'things' you substitute for the letters x, y, z? Multiplying any two 'things', do you always get another 'thing'? If the answers to all these questions are *Yes*, then the set of 'things', α, β, γ, forms a *mathematical group*. If there are any *No* answers, then the 'things' do not form a group. Of course the 'things' must only be considered in the light of the given 'multiplication table' as they do not have any other existence. They can do nothing else but get multiplied. How could the table be *altered* so as to yield some *No* answers to the questions?

The reader should first play by the rules, but he should later attempt to play about with the rules. He may well find some curious structures!

If the reader is put off by the formal look of the game just described, let him instead cut out an equilateral triangle of cardboard and mark the vertices A, B and C. Let him hold it in his hands in a vertical position, with one of the sides resting on the table. Let him now turn the triangle in its own plane about the right-hand vertex resting on the table, until it comes to rest on another side. We can call this the Right move, or R for short. The Left move or L will be similar, but about the other vertex in contact with the table. We still have a third move, which is turning the triangle all the way round until it is back where it started. We can call this the All the Way Round move or A for short. It might be thought that it is rather a waste to move the triangle round, it might just as well be left alone in the first place. Anyone who thought this would be perfectly right.

Do these moves combine always in two's in such a way that two successive moves could have been done in one move? The answer is *Yes*, as is easily verified, and we obtain the table:

A.A = A	A.L = L	A.R = R
L.A = L	L.L = R	L.R = A
R.A = R	R.L = A	R.R = L

It will be easily seen that if A is replaced by α, L by β and R by γ we obtain the same table as before. In fact we could also replace L by γ and then R by β, only A will always have to be replaced by α. The two structures are identical, and what is true of one is also true of the other. Clearly the 'unit element' is A, and the inverses are as follows:

$$A^{-1}=A, \qquad L^{-1}=R, \qquad R^{-1}=L$$

The associative principle of (x.y).z = x.(y.z) is also easily verified by considering all the cases. Cases where some or all the 'moves' in the above formula are the same must naturally also be considered and the identity verified.

As a contrasting example of a structure with three elements which will *not* be a group, the reader is advised to make up the rules of the composition of good, bad and indifferent acts into joint acts. We could say that a good act always leaves us in a good mood, a bad act leaves us in a bad mood and an indifferent act in an indifferent mood. If these three elements make a group, a good act followed by a bad act would be equivalent to a bad act, a bad act followed by a good act equivalent to a good act, and so on.

A card game could introduce a further mathematical group. We could decide that clubs were the 'unit' suit, so that a club card combined with any other suit would result in that other suit. We might say, for example, that if there is a 3 of clubs and a 5 of hearts on the table, these two could be taken by an 8 of hearts, or any cards of the right suit that 'added up' to 8. Two club cards could naturally only be taken by club cards, likewise any two cards of the same suit could be taken by a club card. Further, a heart and diamond could be taken by a spade, a heart and a spade by a diamond, a diamond and a spade by a heart. Jacks, Queens and Kings could count as 11, 12, 13 respectively. Each player would be dealt five cards, and four would be initially placed on the table from the pack. Scoring could be determined by the number of clubs you could make up out of all the cards you have taken, or in any other way. One might count the 'clubs' that can be 'made' out of pairs of diamonds, hearts and spades, nothing over 13 being allowed in any one sum so made. The above game involves the following combination table of suits:

CL.CL = CL	CL.DM = DM	CL.HRT = HRT	CL.SP = SP
DM.CL = DM	DM.DM = CL	DM.HRT = SP	DM.SP = HRT
HRT.CL = HRT	HRT.DM = SP	HRT.HRT = CL	HRT.SP = DM
SP.CL = SP	SP.DM = HRT	SP.HRT = DM	SP.SP = CL

Every suit here is its own inverse, the club is the unit suit, and any pair of suits will combine into some other suit; in addition the associative principle is easily verified, so that the game includes a group with four elements.

This kind of group turns up in many situations. For example, the half-turns about three mutually perpendicular axes would correspond to diamonds, hearts and spades; a whole turn about any axis (or no turn, if it is preferred) to the clubs. This can be verified by turning a book

(a) round a vertical axis through its centre,
(b) round a horizontal axis through its centre parallel to the lines of the printing,
(c) round a horizontal axis through the centre, perpendicular to the lines of printing.

It is best to use two books, one as 'control', i.e. to see how to catch up on the other book which has been moved twice. Of course the two books must be started from the same position.

There will be four positions in which the book can be:

(1) with the front up and the print the right way,
(2) with the front up and the print the wrong way,
(3) with the back up and the print the right way,
(4) with the back up and the print the wrong way.

A half-turn about a vertical axis turns the print round but does not affect whether the front or the back is up. A half-turn about a horizontal axis parallel to the lines of the print changes the side which is showing as well as turns the print round. A half-turn about a horizontal axis perpendicular to the lines of the print changes the side which is showing but leaves the print as it is (i.e. if it is the right way, it stays the right way; if it is the wrong way, it stays the wrong way). The first of these moves is like a spin, the second is a flipping round of the book on to its reverse side either away from you or towards you. The third of them is turning the book over as though you were turning a page (forward or back). The fourth move is, of course, a whole turn or else a no-turn. So if we call the moves

Whole turn = W, Spin = S, Flip = F, and P = Page-turn

we can put the two books in front of us *in the same position*, for example in position (3) of the above four positions. We can then flip and spin our first book, and we shall find it in position (1). How can we get our second book to catch up with the first? We can do the page-turning move. This means that F.S = P. Working out all the possible ways of pairing the moves, we obtain the following table:

W.W = W	W.S = S	W.F = F	W.P = P
S.W = S	S.S = W	S.F = P	S.P = F
F.W = F	F.S = P	F.F = W	F.P = S
P.W = P	P.S = F	P.F = S	P.P = W

which, when compared with the card-game, will be seen to be the same table.

We now have two games with four moves in each, with the same structure. The situation is still fairly closed. There are several ways in which it could be made open, either by retroactive or by progressive analysis, or by application (i.e. practice).

Retroactive analysis could be encouraged by asking whether any 'sub-games' can be found within this game. Is it possible to pick out some moves, so that if you do only these moves pairs of them only combine into these moves again? We could, for example, take (W, S) as such a sub-game; if only W's and S's are combined, only W's and S's are obtained. Likewise (W, F) and (W, P) are possible sub-games.

There could be an even freer form of retroactive analysis. We could ask what exactly makes the game what it is, how could it best be described, without constructing the table? The game can be described as having the following three properties:

(1) The W move when combined with any other move results in that other move,
(2) any move, when done twice, results in the W move,
(3) if we discount the W move, any two of the remaining three result in the third.

It is implicit in these properties that this is a commutative game. It clearly makes no difference which move you do first. Two moves always lead to the same resultant move, in whichever order the moves are made. This is still retroactive analysis in that we are examining a structure and seeing whether or not it has a certain property.

Progressive analysis would consist in attempts to alter or extend the structure. We might ask whether there are any other games with four moves which have different rules. Or we might ask if we can extend the game by introducing further moves. It is not inevitable that every game so constructed will be a mathematical group. In fact, on the contrast principle, some of the games could well be structures without group properties. Here are examples of an alteration, of an extension, and of a structure which is not a group.

Alteration. We could decide to keep the whole rotation and the spin, but abolish the flip and the page-turning. Instead, we could introduce a quarter-left turn and a quarter-right turn. Children usually think of this possibility, but of course they may abolish the spin and the page-turning and keep the flip move, and then extend by having a quarter-flip away from them, and a quarter-flip towards them. If the books they have are thick enough to stand up, they think of this possibility more readily. The table obtained will be as follows overpage:

W.W= W	W.S= S	W.F= F	W.P= P
S.W= S	S.S= W	S.F= P	S.P= F
F.W= F	F.S= P	F.F= W	F.P= S
P.W= P	P.S= F	P.F= S	P.P= W

or

	W	S	L	R
W	W	S	L	R
S	S	W	R	L
L	L	R	S	W
R	R	L	W	S

(where the 'multiplication' signs have been omitted, to give a clearer view of the structure)

It will be seen that this table is essentially different from the last. It has only one sub-game, namely (W, S), instead of three. Also, all pairs consisting of the same move do not combine into the unit move, as they did in the last game, since L.L=S and not W, and R.R=S and not W.

Extension. This could take the form of the introduction of more axes of rotation (it is best to use a square). It is possible to cut out square pieces of cardboard, with a red arrow on one side and a blue arrow on the other (pointing in the same direction), which enable the various positions and moves to be distinguished from one another. All the four lines of symmetry of the square can be used as axes of rotation, keeping still to half-turns for rotations about these axes. It will be discovered that, unless quarter-turns about the vertical axis are introduced, there will be pairs of moves which are not replaceable by any single move. For example, a rotation about a diagonal followed by a flip move could only be done in one move by a quarter-turn, to the right or to the left, depending on which diagonal was used for the first rotation. If rotations about diagonals are introduced, then quarter-turns about the vertical axis will also be necessary. Or is it possible to introduce the quarter-turns without having to introduce the diagonal turns? A quarter-turn and a flip, for example, can only be replaced by a diagonal turn. So it seems that if we want to extend the 'flip, spin, page-turning' game, we must have at least eight moves:

four half-spins about the four lines of symmetry of the square,

two quarter-turns about a vertical axis, one left, one right,

one half-spin about a vertical axis,

one whole spin or no-spin.

It will be instructive to let children construct the 8-by-8 table of this game by using two squares, one for the pair of moves and the other as the control-square for seeing what the pair of moves is equivalent to.

Further extensions can be constructed by rotating cubes about certain sets of axes; but these tend to get rather involved, without the advantage of bringing in any new principle. A little retroactive analysis of our present extension will show that it includes both the 4-move games in it as sub-games. Furthermore, it is not a commutative game, since a flip followed by a quarter-right turn will not yield the same result as a quarter-right turn followed by a flip. The sub-games are naturally commutative, but when we mix the moves in the two 4-move sub-games, we may obtain non-commutative situations.

Non-group. These 5-move games are a good source of discussion for the associative law, the second game being non-associative as well as non-commutative, the first one being both associative and commutative. Here are the tables:

	e	a	b	c	d
e	e	a	b	c	d
a	a	b	c	d	e
b	b	c	d	e	a
c	c	d	e	a	b
d	d	e	a	b	c

	e	a	b	c	d
e	e	a	b	c	d
a	a	e	d	b	c
b	b	c	e	d	a
c	c	d	a	e	b
d	d	b	c	a	e

The first game can be embodied by drawing a circle on the floor and marking five points along the circumference of the circle. Somebody should stand at one of these points, facing towards the centre of the circle. The moves can be as follows:

e = move all the way round the circle (but keep facing the centre)
a = move one space to the left (keep facing centre)
b = move two spaces to the left (keep facing centre)
c = move two spaces to the right (keep facing centre)
d = move one space to the right (keep facing centre).

It should be clear to children by the time they have reached this stage that the quarter-turn game can also be embodied in this way, except that only four points are marked on the circumference of the circle.

The second game is not so easy to embody. It could be played as a card-game, the e's being embodied by Jokers. There being only two Jokers, pairs of cards could be made very valuable if they are of the same suit in any one trick. One glance at the table shows that the game is not commutative as the principal diagonal does not divide the table into two identical halves which are mirror images of each other. For example, $a.b = d$, but $b.a = c$. So in the card-game there would have to be a left-pile and a right-pile for the cards that go on the table to be taken by the players. It is also non-associative, as can be seen by the fact that

$$(a.b).c = d.c = a, \text{ but } a.(b.c) = a.d = c \text{ so that } (a.b).c \neq a.(b.c).$$

This table presents an interesting game since it fails to be a group only because of its non-associativity. It passes on every other count: there is a unit element, e; every element has an inverse, itself; and any pair of elements will lead to another element.

Apart from actually 'playing with' the structures, as in retroactive and progressive analysis, it is possible to look around and discover whether we can see these structures; or if we cannot see them, whether we can make them in different ways. Practice in recognizing or making similar structures is bound to increase our familiarity with what we are doing. Some people are less analytical than others, and for them this is often the only way of obtaining deeper insights. These people will recognize the structures by their 'feel', and it would be foolish to underestimate the effectiveness of this kind of recognition.

Manipulative play with the new structures will help us to become more and more familiar with them. For example, it might occur to someone who has worked out the circular embodiment of the quarter-turn game that it would be possible to turn round and face outwards. This would be a fifth move added to the four in the game. It will soon be clear that this added move leaves the game wide open. We shall have to add three further moves:

(1) go quarter right round the circle, then turn,
(2) go quarter left round the circle, then turn,
(3) go half way round the circle, then turn.

Again we find ourselves with eight moves in the game. Is it the same game as we had before: what sub-games does it have? Or what about adding the turning move to the 5-point circle game? Will it make a 10-move game? Will it be commutative? Can you do the same thing with a 3-point circle game? Will this be a 6-move game? Are there any other 6-move games? If there are, how many? How many 3-move games are there? How many 2-move games? Or 1-move games?

These are questions that are the result of mathematical curiosity being aroused. The urge to find out how things work (retroactive analysis) and to explore new ground (progressive analysis) is very strong in children, and if we put mathematical structures in their hands, they will play with them, extend them and generally mess about with them as they do with their toys.

A few more examples are briefly described below.

Take two children. Stand them up in front of the class. Each child is allowed either to face the class or to have his back to the class. This means that they can assume one of four different positions. Let us call the children Mary and John. We can now have Mary and John performing half-turns, which gives us four moves, namely

(B) Both children turn; (M) Mary turns; (J) John turns; and (N) Nobody turns.

The table of these moves can be calculated by having children actually do the moves, and having a control-pair who would attempt to catch up with John and Mary who will have done two moves. Naturally both pairs must be in the same positions at the start, for example both children in both pairs facing the class. It will be found that this game has the same table as the original card-game, i.e. the same table as the half-turns about three mutually perpendicular axes which were investigated by means of books.

This same group can also be embodied by four children standing at the four corners of a square ABCD, and the moves could be:

(1) Nobody moves;
(2) A and B change, as well as C and D change;
(3) B and C change and A and D change;
(4) A and C change and B and D change.

The first of these games can be extended to an 8-move game by introducing a third child, say Susan. The shorthand form of these eight moves is shown (those children perform a half-turn whose initials are in the move, the rest remaining still). The moves are:

(Nobody), (J), (M), (S), (JM), (MS), (JMS).

It will be found that this game is *not* the same game as the extension of the book-turning game through turning about the diagonals (p. 78). We can, however, extend the 'square dance' by introducing the moves that follow, *in addition* to those already in the dance:

(5) A and C change, others stay still;
(6) B and D change, others stay still;
(7) A goes to B, B goes to C, C goes to D, and D goes to A;
(8) A goes to D, D goes to C, C goes to B, B goes to A.

This will be the same game as the 'book-turning' 8-game.

Yet another 8-move game is generated by marking 8 points at equal distances along the circumference of a circle and introducing the moves:

(1) 1 space to the left;
(2) 2 spaces to the left;
(3) 3 spaces to the left;
(4) diagonally across;
(5) 3 spaces to right;
(6) 2 spaces to right;
(7) 1 space to the right; and finally
(8) move all the way round the circle, or stay where you are.

This game clearly includes the quarter-turn game, as this is obtained by taking the steps (2), (4), (6) and (8). It does not, however, include the card-game. The card-game is naturally included in the extension of the 'square dance', as it has exactly the same rules as the square dance.

An easy 6-move game is obtained by marking 6 points on the circle and having single and double moves to the right and left, as well as a diagonal move and a no-move or all-the-way-round move. This is a commutative game. On the other hand the following 6-move game is not commutative:

Mark three points along a circle A, B, C. Let the following be the moves, assuming that somebody stands at each point:

(L) A goes to C, C goes to B, B goes to A,
(R) A goes to B, B goes to C, C goes to A,
(N) Move all the way round or stay still,
(A) A stays still and B and C change places,
(B) B stays still and A and C change places,
(C) C stays still and A and B change places.

There is a 3-move sub-game, namely (L, R, N), in this game, as well as three 2-move sub-games, namely (N, A), (N, B), (N, C). It will be verified that for example (A).(B) is not the same as (B).(A). One way of playing this game is to have three couples at each of the points A, B and C, a boy and a girl at each point and letting the girls do any two successive moves while the boys stay where they are, after which the boys have to catch up with their partners in one move.[1]

One very important experience which children undergo while playing and manipulating these games is learning the distinction between states and the operators that change these states. In the John and Mary turning game, the positions in which the children are allowed to be are the *states of the game*, the *moves* are the *operators* inducing the transformation of one state into another state. All the games so far introduced, with one exception, are describable as changes of states—in other words, as *transformations*. The one which is not so describable is the non-associative 5-move card-game. A mathematician would immediately prick up his ears at this state of affairs. He would say to himself: 'I wonder if the reason why I cannot find a transformation embodiment of the 5-by-5 table which is non-associative is because there is no such embodiment? How could I ever be sure that I was right? Perhaps all transformations are associative? If they are, then it is impossible for a non-associative table to be described as a set of transformations.' This is the birth of a hypothesis. The playing about with the structures that have associative and non-associative properties, together with groups of transformations, has led him to make a conjecture. He has put his mathematical bricks together in a certain way, and now he wonders if they are going to collapse or stay. How does he find out? He must *analyse* what he has *constructed*. If his hypothesis is wrong, his new structure will collapse as a result of its internal contradictions. If it is right, he hopes to make certain that it is right.

Let us formulate matters more explicitly:

Hypothesis. All games whose moves are able to be described as transformations from one state to another state are associative.

This would mean that the second 5-move game cannot be

[1] This game was used by the author to construct a concept formation task for ten-year-olds. See *Concept formation and personality* Leicester University Press, 1959

so described. In fact, there *do not exist* five definite operations (e, a, b, c and d respectively) acting on any of five states ϵ, α, β, γ and δ, and transforming these into each other, which obey the table.

It is relatively easy to see the associative property of transformations of states from the diagram below. Consider states α, β, γ and δ, and let us use the following notation for the transformations:

$$\alpha \to \beta = X, \quad \beta \to \gamma = Y, \quad \gamma \to \delta = Z, \quad \alpha \to \gamma = U, \quad \beta \to \delta = V$$

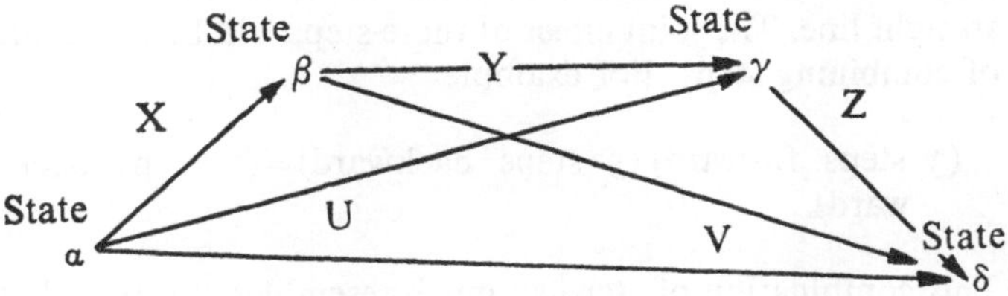

It is clear that X.Y=U and Y.Z=V and that (X.Y).Z= U.Z=$\alpha \to \delta$=X.V=X.(Y.Z). Both ways of grouping the transformations are equivalent to ($\alpha \to \delta$).

However we arrange to combine a series of transformations of states, all such combinations will always be equivalent to a transformation from the first state to the last state. The hypothesis is therefore correct, and thus the *class of transformations* is included in the *class of associative games*, and a non-associative game must lie outside the class of transformations. The enormous time-saving power of such an argument will be appreciated. Without it, we might go on looking for transformation games for a long time to embody our second 5-move table. All this labour is saved by the consideration of the properties themselves of the structures we are playing with. This is another example of progressive analysis, since we progress from the class of associative games and the class of transformation games to the logical relationship that exists between these classes.

The groups we have so far studied in detail are mostly finite groups; that is, they consist of a finite number of elements. The very first example was, however, an infinite group, for there can be as many displacements in space as we like, so that the elements in this group certainly could not be finite in number. The adding of directed numbers provides a one-dimensional example of the group of general displacements. Or if we only wish to consider the adding of positive and negative integers, we must stipulate that there is a smallest or shortest 'move' in terms of which all other moves can be measured. We could for example take steps of uniform length, forward or backward along a straight line. The joint effect of these steps will be the result of combining steps. For example

(3 steps forward).(5 steps backward)=(2 steps backward).

This combination of steps so much resembles addition that instead of our customary dot we might use the plus sign. The 'unit element' in this set is not the 'one step' but the 'no-step'. The inverse of every step is therefore what you would have to do after each step to have the final result of a 'no-step', e.g. the inverse of (4 backward) is (4 forward). Any two steps always combine into another step, there is a unit step, every step has an inverse step; and the procedure *must* be associative, since it is the transformation of states. The states are our positions along the line, the moves up or down the line are the transformations.

Apart from moving up or down a line, we might be turning about an axis *through an angle.* Or we could have somebody moving round a circle, always facing the centre, but allowed to move from any point on the circle to any other point. This is still a group, and it is still commutative. But suppose we introduce the turning move, which allows someone to turn a half-turn while standing on the circumference. To complete the game, we should also have to allow moves such as 'Move x left and turn' or 'Move y right and turn'. We still have a group, but have lost the commutative property. So there are non-commutative infinite groups.

There are a number of instructive types of retroactive analysis that could be done with these games. We might ask in how many ways we could 'map' a game on to an equivalent game. For example we might play the game of dividing numbers by 3 and getting the remainders, then adding the remainders, then if possible again dividing by 3 and getting the remainder and so on. There will only be three possible remainders, 0, 1 or 2. When we add these, we may get a 3 or a 4, but these will turn into a 0 and a 1 respectively upon further division by 3 if what we keep again is the remainder in each case. Denoting the remainders by r_0, r_1 and r_2, we have the table:

$$r_0+r_0=r_0\ ;\ r_0+r_1=r_1\ ;\ r_0+r_2=r_2$$
$$r_1+r_0=r_1\ ;\ r_1+r_1=r_2\ ;\ r_1+r_2=r_0$$
$$r_2+r_0=r_2\ ;\ r_2+r_1=r_0\ ;\ r_2+r_2=r_1$$

If we compare this with the 3-by-3 table of the triangle-turning game, we shall see that we can turn one game into the other by making the following correspondences:

$$r_0 \sim W\ ;\ r_1 \sim L\ ;\ r_2 \sim R$$

or else

$$r_0 \sim W\ ;\ r_1 \sim R\ ;\ r_2 \sim L$$

There are thus two ways in which these games may be 'mapped' on each other. How many ways are there in which the square dance with four moves may be mapped on the card-games? Or the quarter-turn game on to the 4-point circle game? What about the 6-move games? In each case we could map the second game back on to the first game, thereby obtaining a mapping of a game *on to itself.* Each game can be mapped on to itself in a certain definite number of ways, and what is more these mappings themselves could constitute a new game in which the mappings were the moves, and a certain way of 'calling' the various moves were the states. Can any of these mapping-games be themselves mapped on to previously encountered games? It will be found that even this is possible. The mapping games allow us to gain a new insight into the structures, as it shows us once more where the irrelevancies lie. For example in the above 3-move game the mapping shows that there is simply nothing to distinguish a left move from a right move. The left can be called right and the right be called left, and we are still dealing with the identical structure![1]

Another piece of analytical thinking that could be tried, if there were time, is the following. Consider any group with an even number of elements. Is it possible to split the group into a set of pairs as follows:

(i) *Fundamental pairs;* this could consist of the unit element, and one other element, called the transposer, which when applied to itself would yield the unit element.

(ii) *Other pairs;* this would be pairs (x, y) such that when the transposer was applied to x, it yielded y, and when the transposer was applied to y, it yielded x.

Let us see if this is possible with the John-Mary-Susan turning game. The fundamental pair could be:

/(N), (JMS)/—with the move (JMS) being the transposer.

The other pairs would then be:

/(J), (MS)/ ; /(M), (JS)/ ; /(S), (JM)/.

It is clear that the move (JMS) does in fact turn each member of a pair into the other member.

With the simpler John-Mary turning game the pairing could be:

[1] See Van der Waerden, *Modern Algebra*, Springer Verlag, Leipzig, for a fuller account of the elements of groups, particularly Chapter I

/(N), (JM)/ as the fundamental pair and /(J), (M)/ as the other.

These are not the only ways of achieving the splitting into pairs with these properties, and it might be of interest to work out all possible pairings.

The (L), (R), (N), (A), (B), (C) non-commutative 6-game can be paired as follows, the first pair being the fundamental pair:

/(N), (A)/ ; /(L), (C)/ ; /(R), (B)/.

But of course (B) or (C) could equally well have been taken as transposer in the fundamental pair, but not (L) or (R), because (L).(L) is not (N) and (R).(R) is not (N) either. It must be remembered that in this case (A) transposes as a left-hand multiplier. If it is taken as a right-hand multiplier then (B) and (C) must be interchanged in the second and third pairs, i.e. (L) would then be paired with (B) and (R) with (C).

It will be noticed that there is a great similarity between the unit element and the number 1, and between the transposer and the number −1. The other pairs could be regarded as being situated along 'dimensions' different from the 'fundamental dimension' along which the two elements of the fundamental pair are situated. It is these properties of groups with an even number of elements that make them very suitable for defining multiplications in a vector space, as we shall see later on. The complex algebra could be defined as a two-dimensional vector space in which the fundamental dimension would be defined by the fundamental pair (no-move), (half-turn) and the second pair (quarter-turn right), (quarter-turn left). It is clear that the half-turn acts as the transposer, i.e. as the −1, so that vectors can be defined as real multiples of half-turns and of quarter-turns, where the pairs are regarded as independent. Furthermore, equal numbers of half-turns and no-turns cancel out *when added*; similarly, equal numbers of left quarter-turns and right quarter-turns cancel out *when added.* But before it can be made clear to the non-mathematician what is meant exactly by such 'cancelling', the idea of vector space must first be introduced.

Let us consider a set of states, determined by a number of variables such as longitude, latitude, temperature, pressure, humidity, etc. In order to relate these states to each other it is convenient to choose a zero state, and any other state can then be described in terms of the difference between it and this zero state. Taking the first four variables mentioned, we can give the zero state the intersection of the Equator and the Greenwich Meridian at 0°C and 1000 millibars. If we regard East, North, warmer and higher pressure as positive, and West, South, colder and lower pressure as negative, it will be clear that (35, −10, 35, −6) would mean 35° East of Greenwich, 10 degrees South of the Equator, 35°C temperature and 994 millibars pressure, as these would have been the changes necessary to bring us from the zero state to the state in question. Further changes of state could be added on, for example (−5, 12, 2, 14) would mean a change of state involving a displacement 5° West and 12° North, a rise in temperature of 2°C and a rise in pressure of 14 millibars. The resulting state would be a *total* displacement from the zero position of (30, 2, 37, 8), meaning a state of 30° East, 2° North, a temperature of 37°C and a pressure of 1008 millibars. We have added two vectors in a four-dimensional vector space. The vectors are here either states or changes of state (since a state can be decribed as a change from the zero state); addition is the process of superimposition; and the dimensions are the variables.

We can now go on to construct experiences for children to handle whose structure is mathematically identical to a multi-dimensional vector space such as the one above. There must be embodiments for the values of the variables in the various dimensions and these embodiments must have two properties:

(i) they must be independent of each other;
(ii) each representative of a value must have a convincingly recognizable 'opposite', with which, if it occurs together, it is counted as zero, i.e. discounted.

Almost any set of objects will do, so long as there is conventional agreement about which objects count as 'opposites'. I have used matchboxes, large ones and small ones. Sometimes open boxes were the opposites of closed boxes, the large and the small ones indicating two dimensions. At other times, the outsides and the drawers were the opposites; if any drawers occurred together with outsides into which they fitted, it was one of the rules of the game that they had to be put together, laid aside, and not counted towards the pile. The second alternative is the more convincing, since there is a valid reason for discounting the ones that can be put together.

An even better embodiment would be to take a large number of hardboard squares and cut various shapes out of the centres. To each shape there would be the corresponding frame from which it was cut. There would be as many dimensions as the number of different shapes. Children would practise 'counting' how many objects there were in piles, remembering that if any shape could be fitted into a frame, the resulting 'zero-pair' had to be put in a separate pile and not counted. Children would realize that, for example, 4 square frames and 3 triangle shapes could be made up in a great variety of ways, depending on how many zero-pairs they threw into the pile. All such piles would count as the same. Children find the subtraction problems in these situations both amusing and instructive. Suppose we have (2 square frames, 3 circles, 2 triangles, 5 hexagon frames), and we wish to 'subtract' (1 square frame, 4 circles, 2 triangles and 6 hexagons). It is easy to take the 1 square away, as it is plainly there. It is not so easy to take 4 circles from 3, in fact it is palpably impossible except in the conventional way according to the rules of the game. The 3 circles that are on the table may be regarded as 4 circles and 1 circular frame, and from *this* pile (to which the other is equivalent) it is now possible for us to subtract the 4 circles. All the triangles will be removed, leaving none. There are no hexagons at all in the pile and yet 6 must be taken away. Nothing is easier. Just make sure that there are at least 6 pairs of hexagons with their corresponding frames, and the 6 hexagons can then be removed, leaving 6 unpaired hexagon frames, which must be *added* to the 5 hexagon frames already there. So the result of this 'subtraction' is

> (1 square frame, 1 circular frame and 11 hexagonal frames).

It does not take very long for children of eleven or twelve to learn that subtracting something gives the same result as adding its opposite (since this cancels out what we want to subtract), and that adding something is the same as subtracting its opposite. A certain amount of actual manipulation appears to be essential, however, for full grasp of the structure. Its properties are so strange that the corresponding events must be fully lived through or they will never become real for the majority of children.

A certain rough symbolism will grow naturally out of these experiences, and this can be gradually systematized. The incipient symbols will be shorthand notations for the words indicating the objects. For example, cf and c may denote circle frames and circles; sf and s square frames and squares. Soon the relationship between the 'symbols' with f's and those without f's will become apparent. Children will start talking about f-numbers and non-f-numbers, and develop some sort of compromise notation like $\tilde{1}, \tilde{2}, \tilde{3}, \tilde{4}, \tilde{5}$, ... for shapes and $\bar{1}, \bar{2}, \bar{3}, \bar{4}, \bar{5}$, ... for frames. It is possible to omit the abbreviations for the shapes, if a convention is followed about the order used in recording them. One might be dealing with circles, squares, triangles and hexagons. Then

$$(\tilde{2}, \bar{4}, \tilde{3}, \bar{6})$$

could mean 2 circles, 4 square frames, 3 triangles and 6 hexagon frames.

At this stage coloured arrows pointing in the opposite direction might be introduced, up meaning 'twiddle' and down meaning 'bar', on the numbers. One could use three, four or five colours, and do the addition and subtraction exercises with these, on the basis that opposite arrows of the same colour cancel out. The symbols would then become representative in a more abstract way, in that they would symbolize more than one type of situation.

There would be some value in artificial exercises whose purpose is the cutting out of inessential and irrelevant trimmings from the abstractions. These would establish the exact correspondences between different embodiments of the same structure. For example, one could mark a point in the centre of the classroom, and establish directions in which steps might be taken: e.g. (i) towards blackboard; (ii) towards door; (iii) towards windows; and (iv) towards lockers. These could be abbreviated to B, D, W, L. Equal steps could be taken either in the (B, D) direction or in the (W, L) direction, and steps in opposite directions would cancel out. We are obviously dealing with a two-dimensional vector space in which the vectors are sets of steps; previously our vectors were sets of readings on maps, thermometers and barometers, or sets of objects in which opposites had been conventionally agreed upon. To induce children to reach the maximum of abstraction in their formation of this concept, they must discard all irrelevancies and keep the bare bones of the structure. A good way of doing this is to compare the various representations. We might propose the following 'dictionary':

circle ~ step North or B, circular frame ~ step South or D,
square ~ step East or W, square frame ~ step West or L.

Some children could put out an assortment of circles, circular frames, squares or square frames, and others would have to 'translate' this into moving somewhere from the centre of the classroom, with the help of the 'dictionary' key. Others could translate into rises and falls of temperature and pressure, or into John and Mary saving and spending money. For example,

$$\left\{\begin{matrix}\text{2 circles and}\\ \text{3 square frames}\end{matrix}\right\} \sim \left\{\begin{matrix}\text{2 steps B}\\ \text{3 steps L}\end{matrix}\right\} \sim$$
$$\sim \left\{\begin{matrix}\text{2°C rise and}\\ \text{3 m/bars drop}\end{matrix}\right\} \sim \left\{\begin{matrix}\text{John saves 2s.}\\ \text{Mary spends 3s.}\end{matrix}\right\}$$

If further vectors are added, the adding must be a joining, i.e. the steps must be performed from the position already reached. Subtractions could be introduced in terms of the position or state *before* certain things happened. It must be carefully explained that the moves, the rises and falls, etc., are totals; if the position is that John has saved 2s., he may in fact have saved 5s. and then spent 3s. So we can ask the question: (John saved 2s., Mary spent 3s.) – (John spent 3s., Mary spent 2s.). John, clearly, before he spent his 3s. and was left with 2s., must have saved 5s. Likewise Mary, before she spent the 2s. out of the total of 3s. she spent, had spent only 1s., so the answer to this vector subtraction is

(John saved 5s., Mary spent 1s.)

This can be repeated with the objects, with the steps, with the rises and falls in temperatures and pressures, and so on. The similarity of the statements 'before he spent 3s. is the same difference as after he saved 3s.' and 'before the temperature dropped 3°C it was warmer by as much as if it now rose by 3°C' must be realized by children before they can be guided to the appreciation of the underlying structure. The number of dimensions should naturally not be kept to two. When the author once casually mentioned to a class of twelve-year-olds that adults found it difficult to deal with more than three dimensions, they were incredulous, and wondered why numbers after three should suddenly become difficult. Of course, one of the inessential trimmings of the concept of dimension is its spatial representation. Most adults never quite get rid of this, and find 'the fourth dimension' either nonsensical or mystical. The simultaneous handling by children of a fair number of variables does not permit this inhibition to be established. Vector spaces then appear as open structures in which you can have as many dimensions as you like, just as you can have as many objects in a collection as you like.

Once the rule-structure of the concept of a vector space has been appreciated, as well as analysed retroactively, it will come to be regarded as a whole. It can be surveyed, so to speak, from the outside and seen as a whole structure. When this stage has been reached, it should be possible to 'play with' vector spaces as such. Some simple games *with* vector spaces have already been suggested; these took the form of the establishment of correspondences between various representations of a vector space: for example, between the 'space' of steps in the classroom and the 'space' of rises and falls of temperatures and pressures. We could now make these transformations more difficult. Let someone put out a certain number of circles and squares, and their frames, on the table. Let us decide that we are going to record circles and squares as 'twiddle' numbers, and their frames as 'bar' numbers. Let also the B (blackboard) and the W (window) directions be counted as 'twiddle' directions, and the D (door) and L (locker) directions as 'bar' directions. Now consider the following transformation of these objects into steps in the class-room:

$$\left\{\begin{matrix}\text{Number of steps}\\ \text{parallel to BD}\end{matrix}\right\} = 3 \text{ times} \left\{\begin{matrix}\text{Number}\\ \text{of}\\ \text{circles}\end{matrix}\right\} + 4 \text{ times} \left\{\begin{matrix}\text{Number}\\ \text{of}\\ \text{squares}\end{matrix}\right\}$$

$$\left\{\begin{matrix}\text{Number of steps}\\ \text{parallel to WL}\end{matrix}\right\} = 2 \text{ times} \left\{\begin{matrix}\text{Number}\\ \text{of}\\ \text{circles}\end{matrix}\right\} + 3 \text{ times} \left\{\begin{matrix}\text{Number}\\ \text{of}\\ \text{squares}\end{matrix}\right\}$$

Suppose someone has put out 2 circular frames and 5 squares. In the way we have agreed to 'count' these, there are $\bar{2}$ of the circular and $\tilde{5}$ of the square things.

So

Number of steps parallel to BD $=3.\bar{2}+4.\tilde{5}=\bar{6}+\widetilde{20}=\widetilde{14}$

and since twiddles are being counted towards B, the child in the centre must move 14 steps towards the blackboard.

Likewise

Number of steps parallel to WL $=2.\bar{2}+3.\tilde{5}=\bar{4}+\widetilde{15}=\widetilde{11}$

and so our child must take a further 11 steps towards the window.

Mathematical readers may by now be recoiling in horror from the monstrous hybrid which this transformation appears to be. It must be admitted that it is no thoroughbred, but something of a mongrel. The coefficients of the transformations are *natural* numbers, whereas the variables represent *directed* numbers. There is no reason why such readers should not place twiddles on the coefficients, as it is the 'twiddle' numbers that we are going to choose to fulfil the function of positive numbers, the 'bar' numbers being left to act as negative numbers. There is no reason, in fact, why it should not be the other way round; however, a choice has to be made in order to discuss the structures that arise.

When we use numbers, we ignore temporarily all properties of collections except their numbers, i.e. the number of objects that are in them. When we write the figure 5, we are no longer thinking of a collection but of the fact that there are five objects in it. A collection is something you do with objects; that is, you put them together. A number is something you do with collections; that is, you count the objects in them. It is the same with directed numbers. The figure $\tilde{5}$ is no longer a certain number of degrees of temperature, but the result of a count of how many degrees of rise or fall there have been. In the case of the objects, $\bar{2}$ does not actually *denote* the two circular frames; it merely says that there are two of them and that they are frames. This is mathematically an extremely important distinction, as it indicates a shift of level in class-formation.

It should by now be clearer how the multiplication of directed numbers is to be regarded. There are two kinds of multiplication in the algebra of directed numbers:

plain multiplication which multiplies and leaves the *kind* of number as it is

inverting multiplication which multiplies and at the same time inverts the number multiplied into the opposite kind.

We are taking the 'twiddle' numbers as *plain* multipliers, and the 'bar' numbers as *inverting* multipliers. This is why all we have to do to turn the 'mongrel transformation' into a thoroughbred is to put twiddles on the coefficients. These will denote plain multiplications, i.e. multiplications of whatever is there without altering the kind of thing it is. Multiplications by 'bar' numbers will invert as well as multiply. For example $\bar{2}$ times $\tilde{3}$ will not be $\tilde{6}$ but $\bar{6}$. Likewise $\bar{2}$ times $\bar{3}$ will not be $\bar{6}$ but $\tilde{6}$. In the first case the bar multiplications turn a twiddle into a bar, in the second a bar into a twiddle.

This structure does, in fact, occur in practice, as in the saving and spending situation. Let the amount saved per week be denoted by twiddles, the amount spent per week by bars. Let numbers of 'weeks-hence' be denoted by twiddles, and numbers of 'weeks-ago' by bars. Let totals gained be denoted by twiddles and totals spent or lost by bars. If we are spending £3 per week, then 5 weeks ago we had £15 more than we have now, or

$\bar{3}$	$\cdot$	$\bar{5}$	$=$	$\widetilde{15}$
£3 a week spending		5 weeks ago		Total more than now

Speed multiplied by time giving distance is another suitable example, or again any rate of change multiplied by time yielding the total change in the time. These will be enough examples to convince children that the structure is not just something out of a hat.

We can now return to our transformations, armed with the possibility of using either twiddles or bars for the coefficients. We can thus re-write the transformation in the following way:

Let X denote the number of steps in the (B, D) direction, Y the number of steps in the (W, L) direction, we have

$$X = \tilde{3}.(\quad\quad) + \tilde{4}.[\quad]$$
$$Y = \tilde{2}.(\quad\quad) + \tilde{3}.[\quad]$$

where the round brackets will enclose the number of circles, and the square ones the number of squares, that we are putting on the table.

Let only one part of the class see what is on the table. This part quietly works out where the child has to go from the centre of the room, in accordance with the transformation of objects into steps. The objects are then removed, and all traces of calculation too, and the other half of the class now has to find out what was on the table. It is best to start this 'guessing game' with simple vectors, so that success can be achieved after a few guesses; these are checked by putting them through the mill of the transformation. The vectors can get harder and harder to guess, until someone will ask whether there is some more systematic way of finding out what was on the table. After all, if the steps can be *calculated* from the things, why must the things be *guessed* from the steps? Cannot the things be also *calculated* from the steps? The children are now beginning to talk *about* the transformation, instead of just working it. They are wondering how the transformation could be *inverted*. To think in this way, they must have constructed a whole image of the transformation. Just as transformations are done to spaces, so inversions are done to transformations. We are about to change levels again.

To help children through these difficulties, we might

proceed like this. We first choose our 'currency' to represent the counting of objects in the vectors. We might have green and red counters, or live and dead matches. Suppose that we use green counters as we have used twiddles, and red counters as we have used bars. We must also have a number of large circles and large squares, cut out of cardboard or something more durable. On each large circle we shall put the *number* of counters indicating the *number* of circles in our vector, on each large square we shall put the *number* of counters indicating the *number* of squares in our vector. The transformation on page 98 will now be represented in concrete fashion as shown below:

Box for number of steps along BD =

Box for number of steps along WL =

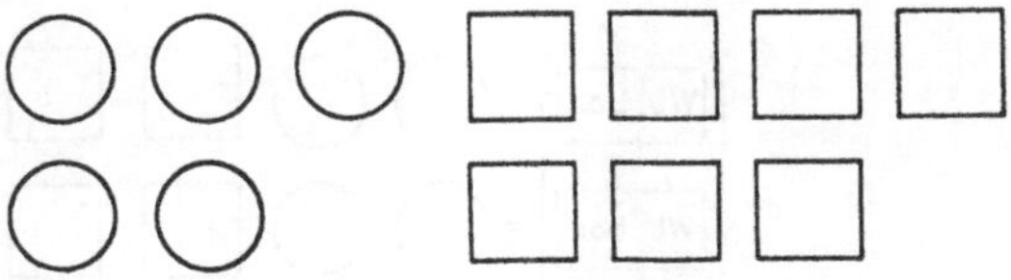

When every circle and square has had its counters put on it, depending on the vector involved, the counters can be collected and put in the appropriate boxes. Pairs of red and green counters can be emptied out, and what is left will give the number of steps needed. Green will be towards B or W, red towards D or L, depending on the box.

This particular transformation is perhaps a difficult one to start on. For example, if instead of 3 squares there were 4 squares in the second row, somebody might well suggest that to get the number of counters to be put on one circle you had to subtract the contents of the WL box from the contents of the BD box. Assuming that such easy examples have already been given, it can be suggested that an attempt be made to turn this example into such an easy one. A little help may be necessary here, unless the children have already been trained in 'mathematical daring'. It could be pointed out that two BD boxes full of the appropriate number of counters would be obtained by emptying the counters from 6 large circles and 8 large squares.

Similarly three WL boxes full of the appropriate number of counters would be obtained by the emptying of the counters from 6 large circles and 9 large squares. These 'multiplications' should in fact be carried out with the appropriate receptacles, but without any counters, and the following arrangements would be obtained:

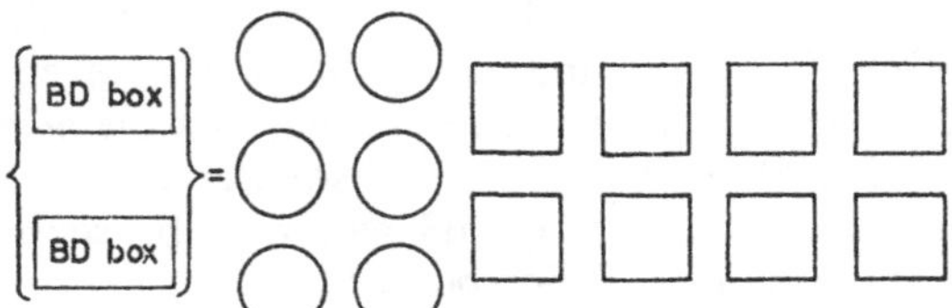

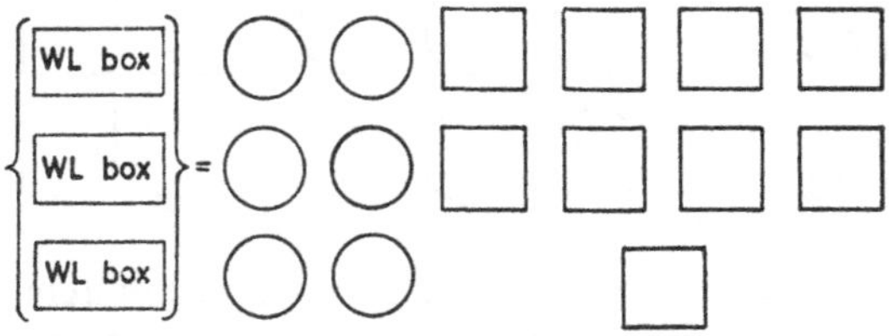

It is now not difficult to see that whatever needs to be put on one large square is obtained by subtracting the contents of two BD boxes from three WL boxes. Supposing we put 5 circular frames and 3 squares on the table. It is easily calculated that 3 red counters go in the BD box and 1 red counter in the WL box. In other words, the child in the centre of the room takes 3 steps towards the door, then 1 step towards the lockers. Suppose we now remove the 'objects' from the table. The rest of the class must find out what they were by what the child does in moving away from the centre of the room. It will be easy to translate the steps into red counters in the respective boxes. But we now know that

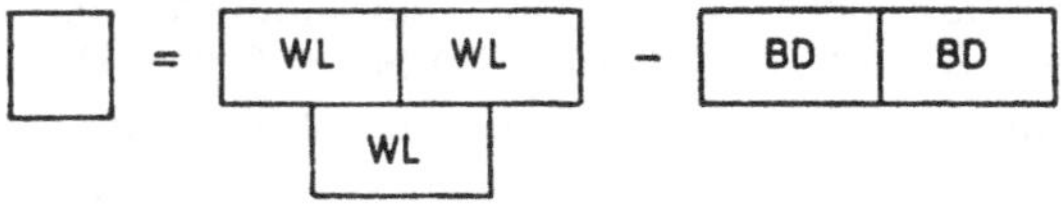

so the contents of one large square will be

$$3.(\text{contents of WL box}) - 2.(\text{contents of BD box})$$
$$= 3.\ (1\ \text{red}) - 2.(3\ \text{red}) = 3\ \text{red} - 6\ \text{red} = 3\ \text{green}$$

and the number of squares on the table will be 3, as the green counters were to denote objects and the red ones their frames.

Even if help has been given to get children to reach this point, they should certainly be left free now to discover just how many circles there must have been. They may look at the transformed transformations or at the original ones. It is easy to see from the second equation of the original transformation that if the WL box has 1 red in it, and the three large squares altogether 9 green (as we now know that each one must have 3 green on it), we must add 10 red to the 9 green to obtain the one red in the box, and so the two large circles must account for 10 red, in other words each circle must have 5 red on it. This gives us our 5 circular frames with which the first half of the class tried to puzzle the other half. Eventually the inverse equation will be written as

$$\square = \bar{2}.X + \tilde{3}.Y$$

and the corresponding expression for the large circle will likewise be expressed in symbolic form. If it is done in this way, then the children have not only had their first experience of the solution of simultaneous equations, but they have started inverting 2-by-2 transformations or matrices. This is a good opportunity to introduce degenerate transformations that do not have inverses, such as for example:

$$X = 2x + 3y$$
$$Y = 6x + 9y$$

which is the application of the contrast principle. If this is the transformation that is given for turning objects into steps, then there will be an awful lot of places on the classroom floor which will be out of bounds while these transformations are being used. It is clear that whatever objects we put on the table, the relationship $Y=3X$ will always hold between the steps. So if the WL displacement is not 3 times as much as the BD displacement, we could look for ever for objects from which such a set of steps could have arisen, but we shall never find any such set of objects. The 'object-space' has been translated not into the whole floor, but into a line along the floor, whose equation in Cartesian co-ordinates is $Y=3X$.

There are many other avenues to follow from here. The number of dimensions could be increased and inverses found (care should be taken that the determinants of the transformations given to children in the beginning have determinant 1 or -1, so that any whole number of steps can be turned back into a whole number of objects on the table). Determinants could be introduced as functions that determine whether a transformation is degenerate or not. Values of λ could be found such that for example

$$\begin{aligned} ax+by&=\lambda x \\ cx+dy&=\lambda y \end{aligned}$$

should have non-zero solutions in (x, y), where a, b, c, d are given constant coefficients determining the transformation. The solution of this problem leads to the transformation of the general quadratic function in two variables into a sum or difference of squares, a procedure of fundamental importance both in geometry and in dynamics, not to mention the solution of quadratic equations and the appreciation of their structure. Intelligent twelve-year-olds will take to these problems with alacrity, thereby acquiring a taste for really tough mathematical thinking, before the boredom with endless formal manipulations overtakes them. There is no space in this small volume to go into all the exciting possibilities that the mathematical game opens up for children and adults alike, but it seems that they are almost limitless. What is being suggested is simply that the type of game which the research mathematician plays with his apparently austere toys should be translated to the level of secondary school children, thereby giving them a taste and so almost certainly a liking for this most exciting and most human of all games: building up and playing with mathematical structure.

4

The Mathematical Story

IN THIS chapter we shall be concerned with ways of facilitating the manipulation of imagery, and particularly mathematical imagery. Whenever we think, we do not do so *in vacuo*, but in terms of images. These images need not be visual; they may be auditory, tactile or even olfactory. My son came home the other day and declared that there was a French smell in the house; clearly some olfactory imagery had become associated with situations that had been classified as French. Our process of thinking is accompanied by a whole chorus of rapidly changing imagery in several sense-modalities. When we reason, we consciously try to transform certain images into others with given properties. In mathematics such imagery has usually been considered an impediment, in that it clutters up our thinking with irrelevancies. In actual fact the conscious manipulation of images may well be a help towards more effective mathematical thinking.

Along with the development of an abstraction, there is an accompanying development of the corresponding imagery. When a situation is considered in isolation, i.e. *in concreto*, the accompanying imagery is very detailed. When we think of a particular event (say, the occurrence of an accident) we picture the scene in all its details. When we speak of accidents as a class of events, we have a much greyer image, stripped of particular features. This greying or stripping of the imagery is one of the consequences of the application of the principle of multiple embodiment, as by it the formation of the abstraction at which the embodiments are aimed is artificially accelerated. The development of an abstraction requires, however, a great deal more than the stripping of irrelevant imagery. As we have seen, at certain stages of the learning cycles analysis of a retroactive or progressive kind is necessary in order to consolidate the abstraction and to make sure that it is available as a 'plaything' with which to start another cycle. This analysis consists in making sure how the existing pieces fit together, or how they may be related to something new. In either case, manipulation of the constituent parts according to the rules present in the abstraction (rule-bound play) is necessary before fully conscious analysis of the situation can be achieved. In the last chapter we studied some examples of how such rule-bound games can be played with representative objects, on which the rule-structure is artificially and arbitrarily imposed. It is also possible to invent imaginary situations involving the same rule-structures, as we have seen in the story of the magician's castle. The saving-spending story, the ship's swimming pool and so on, are other, much simpler versions. In these, only a small part of the whole structure is embodied, whereas the magician's town is adapted to the whole theory of indices and even to the introduction of the differential calculus. The wider the scope of a story, the more suitable a tool it is for the practice of image-manipulation, which ought to be the counterpart of symbol-manipulation. When we talk about the 'meaning' of a symbol, we refer to the kind of image that comes to our mind. When we come across the word-symbol *tree*, we form the image of a tree. Suppose we read 'the tree has been cut down', we then transform the image corresponding to 'tree' to one of a 'cut-down tree'. By saying that we understand, we mean that we have carried out a transformation of imagery corresponding to the symbols.

Symbol-manipulation in mathematics is all too often utterly meaningless simply because there is no corresponding transformation of images. When we see

$$x^2+2x+1 \text{ and later } (x+1)^2$$

very few of us experience an image-transformation, though we may form an image of a teacher writing on a blackboard. The mathematical story has the purpose of making children adept at image-transformation. Once facility is achieved in such transformations, they can be expressed by means of a symbolic system, which sooner or later develops into conventional mathematical symbolism.

Practically any part of mathematics can be represented by a story. To bring out the parallelism, I shall give stories whose structures are mathematically identical to the games described in the last chapter. A good knowledge of a mathematical structure should enable any teacher to invent corresponding stories; alternatively, the invention of stories could make fascinating homework for children who have been studying a structure.

Of the stories which follow, the first have the structures of multi-dimensional vector spaces. The next ones include some of the group-properties described in the last chapter, and these lead to representations of real, complex and hypercomplex algebras.

Vector-space stories

(1) *The dance story.* In a dance-hall the proprietor makes the following rules:

(a) One is only permitted to dance with the opposite sex.
(b) Adults are only allowed to dance with adults, and children with children.
(c) While the band is playing, everybody must dance if they can find someone with whom they are allowed to dance.
(d) Anyone without a dancing partner must go into the refreshment room and wait there.

Various problems may be posed. Suppose that there are 2 girls and 3 men in the refreshment room, and 3 boys and 3 men come in. Who will remain in the refreshment room? The answer is obviously 1 boy and 6 men, as the 2 girls already there will dance with 2 of the 3 boys who come in.

Again it is possible to subtract children who are not in the refreshment room but on the dance-floor. For example, if there are 3 boys and 2 men in the refreshment room, and suddenly 5 boys and 5 men are needed to do an urgent repair, it will be necessary to fetch a further 2 boys and 3 men from the dance-floor, in addition to the ones who are waiting in the refreshment room. The partners of those who have been fetched will now have to go to the refreshment room. This means that there will be 2 girls and 3 women left in the refreshment room. Symbolically we write this as

(3 boys and 2 men) − (5 boys and 5 men) = (2 girls and 3 women)

Subtractions can always be carried out, assuming that enough couples are dancing on the dance-floor.

This story embodies a two-dimensional vector space. The two dimensions are the children and the adults, the opposite 'objects' being the opposite sexes. The vectors are represented by the people in the refreshment room at any one moment, and the zero-class is the dance-floor. It is easy to add to the number of dimensions by, for example, introducing old men and old women. If four dimensions are required, children, teenagers, men and women, old men and old women, would supply the need.

In order to prevent too close a link between the developing image-manipulation and the final abstract structure, it might be advisable to interchange the roles of age and sex relationships, as in the following story:

(2) *The boating-lake story.* The proprietor of a boating lake makes the following rules:

(a) Any child is allowed on the premises provided he is willing to be taught to row by an adult of the same sex. Any adult is allowed in likewise if he or she is willing to teach a child of the same sex to row.

(b) Any person who has anyone with whom he can go rowing must do so. Every boat must have an adult and a child in it, and they must be of the same sex.

(c) Any person who cannot find anyone with whom to go rowing must go to the swimming pool and wait there.

It will be seen that the same two-dimensional structure is represented here as in the last story, except that males and females now represent the two dimensions, and adults and children the opposite 'directions' of the same dimension. Adding and subtracting can be done as before, the vectors being the people waiting in the swimming pool, and the zero-class being the people boating on the lake. To help children identify the two stories and become aware of their common structure, they can be asked to transform dance-floor problems into boating-lake problems and vice versa.

Saving-spending situations can be introduced where two or more people are saving and/or spending *independently* of each other. For example the following would be an addition in a representation of a three-dimensional vector space:

(J. saves 2s., M. spends 3s., S. spends 1s.) + (J. spends 3s., M. spends 2s., S. saves 3s.) = (J. spends 1s., M. spends 5s., S. saves 2s.)

Subtractions can be given by suggesting what each person would have had if they had not spent or saved certain specified amounts. If there is confusion between states and operators, it should be pointed out that a zero state is chosen in which nobody has anything (although there is no actual reason why some other zero state should not be chosen), and any operator naturally gives the state reached when it is applied to the zero state.

All these representations should be related to each other, by asking children to transform problems from one story to the other and then to solve them in each representation, until the mathematical equivalence of them all begins to take shape. For bright children this will not present any difficulty; in fact, they will delight in their developing agility in being able to transform problems into equivalent problems. For the less well-endowed child, such a process will represent real hard work, but the reward is great when insight into the structure is achieved. This sort of enrichment of experience is, in fact, the only way to ensure that below-average children attain and enjoy the same abstractions as their more fortunate brothers and sisters.

Algebra stories

It is easy to restrict oneself to one dimension by having children only (or adults only) in the dance story, and males only (or females only) in the boating-lake story. We have seen that it is equally easy to increase the number of dimensions indefinitely. In the construction of algebras it is possible to start with a vector space with any number of dimensions, but it is wiser not to start with more than two dimensions, and some teachers will no doubt prefer to start with one dimension only. Let me first give an 'embellishment' of the one-dimensional story which is necessary to turn it into the usual algebra of directed numbers.

(a) *Dance story.* Suppose that one night children only are allowed to come and dance. Otherwise the normal rules apply. In that case, there can never be a boy and a girl in the refreshment room, because they would be dancing. But suppose that there is a long line of people waiting at the entrance to come in; the proprietor might decide to exchange the people who are in the refreshment room for some of the people who are waiting outside. The proprietor has lots of children of his own, and he tells them to organize the change-over. They think out the following rules:

(i) If one boy announces the change, for every boy that goes out another boy must come in; for every girl that goes out one girl must come in. If n boys announce the change, for every child that goes out, n children of the same sex must come in.

(ii) If n girls announce the change, for every child that goes out, n children of the opposite sex must come in.

In this situation the boys represent the positive integers

and the girls the negative integers. In the vector-space story there was no way of distinguishing positive from negative integers, as the roles of the boys and the girls were entirely symmetrical. Now that 'multiplication' has been introduced, this is no longer so. When the boys announce the change, the result is the keeping of the sexes as they are (but possibly multiplying them); the girls induce a change of sex as well as a possible multiplication (if more than one girl does the announcing).

Divisions can be carried out by giving the final total and either the previous number of people in the refreshment room or the number of announcers. In this situation the commutative law is not at all obviously true. For example, would one necessarily expect that 2 girls operating on 3 boys in the refreshment room would yield the same set of people at the tables of the refreshment room as 3 boys operating on 2 girls? Under the present rules the commutative law is true, but it would be very easy to change the rules so that it was no longer true. We could have boy x boy = boy, girl x girl = girl, girl x boy = boy, boy x girl = girl.

It would be fruitful from the mathematical point of view to play about with the rule-structure in this way. What price do we have to pay for such a daring innovation? The associative law is certainly true for such a multiplication. But what about the distributive law? Is it true that

$$A \times (B+C) = AxB + AxC \text{ for all A, B, and C?}$$

A class can usefully discuss the zero-operator. Multiplication by zero ought to yield zero, and there should be a form of announcement which clears everyone out of the refreshment room without letting anyone else in. It was suggested in one class that there should be a tape-recorder which could be turned on to announce that everyone must leave, as it was closing time. The tape-recorder does away with a human announcer; that is, a zero number of children do the announcing, and the result is that all must go. It will be appreciated that zero operating on 5 boys is a very different situation from 5 boys operating on zero, i.e. on an empty refreshment room. But of course the result is the same in both cases, namely an empty refreshment room. So the prosaic relations

$$0 \times 5 = 5 \times 0 = 0$$

acquire quite a novel significance as a result of the image-manipulation.

(b) *Boating-lake story.* Suppose that boys and men are the only people allowed in the boating lake one day. Boys and men in the management can announce the change-over of those lounging in the swimming pool waiting for a chance to row. One might agree that, if a boy announced the change, for every boy leaving the pool another boy must come in; for every man, another man. If a man announced the change, for every boy leaving the pool a man must come in; for every man leaving it a boy must come in. The same convention as before would be observed if several boys or men announced a change.

(c) *Saving-spending story.* The savings and spendings could be weekly savings and spendings, the multipliers could be the number of weeks in the future or the past, the products the total gain or loss over the total period.

This is no longer a 'unitary' story, since the numbers do not everywhere count the same things. We need a certain amount of awareness of the fact that it is not the 'objects' or the 'people' that are multiplied but the *numbers* of such 'objects' or 'people', before this story can be regarded as being on the same footing as the other stories. Take a transformation like:

3 girls announce change for 4 girls in refreshment room, = 12 boys in the refreshment room

into

If we are spending 3s. weekly, 4 weeks ago we should have had 12s. *more* than now.

This is quite a difficult feat, yet it is an essential test of abstraction. It is the free passage between isomorphic representations of the same mathematical structure which proves that the structure has become operational through having become abstract.

Let us now turn to two-dimensional vector spaces. We shall only treat the dance story, and the reader can transform the boating-lake story in a similar manner.

(d) *Two-dimensional dance story* (*first structure*). Let us have the adults and the children back at the dance, thereby introducing two dimensions again. The problem is how to arrange the change-overs. There are now four different kinds of people:

boys	girls	first dimension	(AGE)
men	women	second dimension	
first sense	second sense		
(SEX)			

The dimensions differ from one another by *age*, the senses differ from one another by *sex*. We might for example assign the following properties to these people as *operators*, i.e. as people standing up and announcing the change-over:

Boy: no change
Man: change of age
Girl: change of sex
Woman: change of age and sex.

If a man announces the change-over, men are exchanged for boys and boys for men, women for girls and girls for women. If a woman announces it, men are replaced by girls and girls by men, boys by women and women by boys. It will be seen that the boy and the girl still have the same role as in the one-dimensional dance story, but they operate over an extended field. For example, a girl announcer can exchange a man for a woman.

It will be instructive to develop the table resulting from the operation of one person on one person. There are sixteen possibilities, and they can be summed up in the following table:

	boy	girl	man	woman
boy	boy	girl	man	woman
girl	girl	boy	woman	man
man	man	woman	boy	girl
woman	woman	man	girl	boy

The people shown in the left-hand column are the operators or announcers, the people shown in the top row are the people in the refreshment room when the announcement is made. The table shows who will be in the refreshment room after the exchange has taken place. It will be seen that the operators and the operands could be inverted, i.e. A operating on B = B operating on A. In other words, the table is commutative. It is in effect the same table as the card-game produced in the last chapter.

If more than one person is operating, each person must have his effect on the final state of the refreshment room, according to the rules developed. For example if there are

(2 girls and 1 man) announcing the change, while there are (2 boys and 3 men) in the refreshment room

the total effect is calculated as the sum of the partial effects, i.e. the 2 girls will effect an exchange of the 2 boys and 3 men into 4 girls and 6 women, the 1 man will effect an exchange of the 2 boys and 3 men into 2 men and 3 boys. When the possible partners have gone dancing there will be 1 girl and 4 women left in the refreshment room. Symbolically:

$$(2g + 1m).(2b + 3m) = 1g + 4w$$

It will be seen that this structure cannot be the same as that of the complex algebra. The boy clearly plays the role of 1, and the girl plays the role of -1. The boy has four different square roots (see diagonal of table), and the girl has none (this is not evident from the table, as there might be some other composite square roots, but it is not difficult to show that there are no square roots of a girl, even if fractional or irrational parts of people are allowed!). It is, however, a similar structure. The algebra corresponding to this story can be symbolized by putting $i^2 = 1$ instead of $i^2 = -1$ as in the complex algebra. The man can be denoted by i and the woman by $-i$, so that the transformation above can be symbolized more simply by writing

$$(-2+i).(2+3i) = -1-4i, \text{ assuming } i^2 = 1$$

One interesting feature of this structure is that A times B can be zero without either A or B being zero.

Put $A = 1 + i$ and $B = 1 - i$, and we have A times $B = 0$.

In the language of our story this means that if a boy and a man announce a change-over and there are just a boy and a woman in the refreshment room, there will be nobody in the refreshment room when the exchange has taken place and everyone has gone dancing who can. The boy's announcement will result in a boy and a woman, the man's announcement will result in a man and a girl. Clearly the boy and the girl will go dancing, and so will the man and the woman.

It is an interesting project to get children to find all the possible ways in which the refreshment room can be emptied. It can always be emptied by putting in a zero set of announcers—for example, 2 men and 2 women. Whoever is in the refreshment room, such a set of announcers will always clear it. But what we have found is a somewhat more cunning way of achieving a clearance, and this leads naturally to the study of 2-by-2 determinants, as the mathematical reader will realize.

(e) *Two-dimensional dance story* (*second structure*). It will be realized that the set of rules given as the definition of the structure of the last story is not the only possible one. If an open-ended problem is desired, the situation can be thrown wide open and children asked to provide different sets of rules. Each set of rules can be investigated, and an aesthetic evaluation in terms of elegance may be attempted. With a little guidance here and there, it is not difficult to get children to construct rules which yield the structure of the complex algebra.

The rules are as follows. The boy and the girl operators may be left the same as they are in the first structure (although this is not essential). The man and woman operators will be as follows:

Man: children are exchanged for adults of the same sex, adults for children of the opposite sex.

Woman: children are exchanged for adults of the opposite sex, adults for children of the same sex.

Using b, g, m, w for boy, girl, man and woman, we have the following table:

	b	g	m	w
b	b	g	m	w
g	g	b	w	m
m	m	w	g	b
w	w	m	b	g

It will be seen that replacing b by 1, g by -1, m by i, and w by $-i$, we obtain the multiplication table current in the complex algebra, provided $i^2 = -1$:

	1	−1	i	−i
1	1	−1	i	−i
−1	−1	1	−i	i
i	i	−i	−1	1
−i	−i	i	1	−1

In this way we have reproduced the quarter-turn game of the last chapter. But we have done more than that. We have inserted the quarter-turn game into a two-dimensional vector space, the quarter-turn game providing the rule-structure for the multiplication. There are four unit vectors in a two-dimensional vector space, and so the multiplication table will have to be a 4-by-4 table. There are two, and only two, really elegant 4-by-4 tables that correspond to 4-element mathematical groups. The two algebras we have constructed are built up with the aid of these two mathematical tables. Any *other* algebras we might construct from a two-dimensional vector space, and with some *other* 4-by-4 table, will prove to be less elegant.

It would be interesting to prove that, in the complex algebra, if $A \times B = 0$, then either A or B must be zero. This makes the complex algebra even more elegant than our first structure. In obedience to the contrast principle, at least one contrast algebra should be constructed beside the complex algebra. In fact, in order to appreciate the elegance of the structures just sketched, children should be allowed to 'mess around' with other, rather more 'pathological', algebras. They will then appreciate the mathematical finesse which characterizes the more carefully thought-out structures.

(f) *Three-dimensional dance story.* Let us consider the dance now with children, teenagers and adults, with the aid of the diagram opposite:

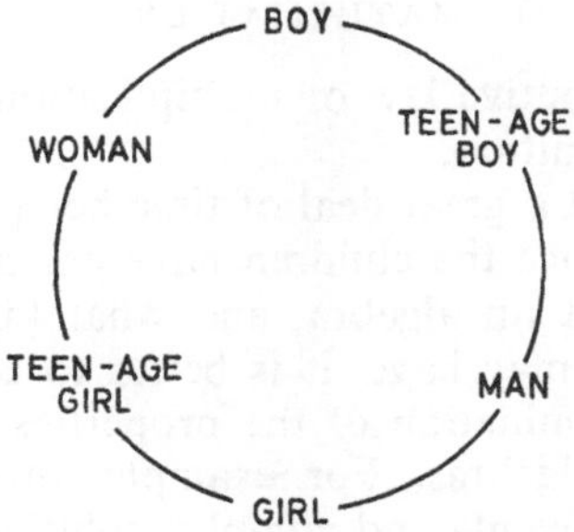

MULTIPLICATION CLOCK

We can introduce the following rules for the operators:

boy:	no change
girl:	change of sex
teenage boy:	exchange for person one step clockwise on the clock
teenage girl:	exchange for person two steps counter-clockwise on the clock
man:	exchange for person two steps clockwise on the clock
woman:	exchange for person one step counter-clockwise on the clock

If more than one operator announces the change-over, the total effect is again calculated as the sum of the partial effects. For example $(2tg+m)$ operating on $(b+tb+3w)$ would be $(2tg+2w+6g)$ as from 2tg, and $(m+g+3tb)$ as from m, which together will yield $(w+7g+1tb)$ left in the refreshment room after all those who must go dancing have gone.

A four-dimensional algebra could be built up out of any of the 8-move games given in the last chapter and be similarly investigated.

It must now be clear that, from any vector space of n dimensions and a mathematical group of 2n elements, it is possible to build up an n-dimensional algebra. If the unit vectors are grouped in opposite pairs $(\tilde{e}_1, \bar{e}_1)$, $(\tilde{e}_2, \bar{e}_2)$ . . . . $(\tilde{e}_n, \bar{e}_n)$, a 2n-by-2n multiplication table will determine the rule-structure. The distributive law of multiplication is, of course, stipulated by definition.

It is not suggested that a great deal of time be spent on constructing algebras. Once the children have grasped the idea of how to construct an algebra, and what kinds of properties such algebras may have, it is better to concentrate on the detailed examination of the properties of the real and the complex algebras. For example, quadratic equations with real coefficients and complex solutions can be introduced through the dance story and other embodiments. The equation

$$x^2+2x=-2$$

can be put in the context of the story as follows:

'There are a lot of twins in the proprietor's family. One day, some of the proprietor's children happened to be in the refreshment room when the change was announced by their identical twins and by 2 other boys. After the change, when all possible couples had gone dancing, there remained 2 girls in the refreshment room. Who was in the refreshment room before the change-over? (NB. The proprietor may have grown-up children as well.)'

The solutions to the problem are:

either (i) a girl and a man
or (ii) a girl and a woman.

In the first case, the announcers must have been a girl, a man and 2 boys. These would have the same effect as a man and a boy, because the girl and one boy would have the effect of clearing the room. It is enough, therefore, to calculate the effect of the other boy and of the man. The boy operating on the girl and the man produces a girl and a man; the man will produce a woman and a girl (adults have to be exchanged for children, but of the opposite sex!). The man and the woman will go dancing, and two girls will be left as required. Similarly it can be shown that a girl and a woman will also yield a solution to the problem.

It is easy to devise a more concrete form of the structure to enable children to manipulate the situation physically and not only in their imagination. Four colours are selected and objects such as counters or the like provided in these colours. They can be arranged in a two-dimensional vector space by stipulating that, for example, a green and a red cancel out, and a blue and a yellow cancel out. Then three boxes could be provided marked respectively:

(a) Vector, (b) Operator, (c) Result.

It must be decided what effects the various coloured objects will have when used as operators on other objects used as vectors. One might have the following rules:

green: leaves everything unaltered (as the operator 1)

red: turns everything into its opposite (as the operator -1)

blue: turns green into blue, blue into red, red into yellow, and yellow into green (as the operator $+i$)

yellow: turns green into yellow, yellow into red, red into blue, and blue into green (as the operator $-i$)

The equation $x^2+2x=-2$ would look like this now:

To be determined	.	Whatever is in operator + 2 green	=	2 red
Operator box		Vector box		Result box

There are two solutions:

either (i) a red and a blue
or (ii) a red and a yellow.

Notice that, although the problem is stated in terms of green and red objects only, the solutions involve blue and yellow objects. This is like the dance story, where the problem was put in terms of children only but we needed adults to solve it.

Exercises of this sort lead children to the important

mathematical activity of extending the field of operations; that is, to acts of generalization.

If a spatial representation is desired, the green and the red objects may be replaced by up and down arrows such as

$$\uparrow \quad \text{and} \quad \downarrow$$

the blue and the yellow objects by right and left arrows such as

$$\rightarrow \quad \text{and} \quad \leftarrow$$

In this case we could take $\uparrow$ as the unit operator corresponding to $+1$, and $\downarrow$ as the opposite of this operator, i.e. as the one corresponding to -1. Also $\rightarrow$ could be blue and $\leftarrow$ could be yellow. The operators would now have the following effects:

$\uparrow$ leaves everything unaltered (as operator $+1$)
$\downarrow$ turns everything into its opposite (as operator -1)
$\rightarrow$ turns everything clockwise through a right angle
$\leftarrow$ turns everything counterclockwise through a right angle.

Our equation would now look like this:

?	·	$? + \uparrow\ \uparrow$	=	$\downarrow\ \downarrow$
Operator box		Vector box		Result box

The solutions are, of course:

either (i) $? = \downarrow + \rightarrow$
or (ii) $? = \downarrow + \leftarrow$

Since we know that the complex algebra is a commutative one, the same solutions would be obtained if we interchanged what we put in the operator and the vector boxes.

The combination of such physically realized situations, which can be physically manipulated and explored, and the imaginary situations provided by a mathematical story, yield the most effective learning situations. Both the stories and the physical situations can be further complicated by the admission of fractional components of the vectors. In this way we shall continue to engage children's interest in unravelling further the emerging mathematical structures. It will be apparent from the children's reactions to the ways problems are formulated whether or not they are ready to consider the properties of pure structure independently of its embodiment. If the problem of obtaining zero from non-zero factors is put to them in terms of the story, i.e. by asking how the refreshment room can be cleared without opposite sets of children doing the announcing, they often reply in terms which leave out all reference to the story. This stage is usually accompanied by the free use of symbolism, which by now has become a way of communicating information about a structure. The corresponding imagery has been stripped of its irrelevancies. Reaching this stage should be the aim of all enlightened mathematics teaching.

As suggested in the last chapter, there are many mathematical roads that can be followed once the idea of a vector space is grasped, and the construction of algebras is only one of these. The consideration of linear sub-spaces would lead to linear equations; the transformation of spaces into other spaces would lead to matrix theory, and this in turn has an enormous number of applications quite within the comprehension of the secondary school child. We next describe a story structured according to the properties of a four-dimensional vector space based on the algebra of positive and negative integers. Once the structure has been understood, there is no need for the restriction of the basis-algebra to positive and negative integers. Even a complex basis-algebra can be represented by modifying the story slightly.

The hamster—mouse—guinea pig farm

There is a farmer who breeds a great number of pet hamsters, mice and guinea pigs. He knows that children like playing with such pets, and he provides two rooms for this purpose. At the entrance to the first room, which is a square one, children find a hatch where they can ask for animals to play with. They must, however, observe the following rules:

(a) Nobody may play with more than 3 animals at the same time.
(b) Nobody may play with more than one of each kind of animal at the same time.
(c) Children can come in and simply watch, if they do not want to be responsible for any animals.
(d) Any pair of children who *between them* have exactly one mouse, one hamster and one guinea pig (i.e. no more and no less than this) must both go over to the round room, which is next to the square room, and play there.

According to these rules, eight possibilities may occur. A child may go in without any animals, he may go in with one animal (this can occur in three ways), he may go in with two animals (this can also occur in three ways), or he may go in with three animals, which can only be one mouse, one guinea pig and one hamster. The children are paired off into 'opposite' pairs as follows:

(No animal: three animals),
(Mouse: Hamster and Guinea pig),
(Hamster: Mouse and Guinea pig),
(Guinea pig: Mouse and Hamster).

Any such pairs have to leave the square room and play in the round room.

In order to provide the basis-algebra, which up to now is that of the natural numbers (not usually designated 'algebra' by mathematicians), we can add to the story as follows. As the children get their animals they are given a ticket, on which is written what animals they are taking from the hatch. Every child must have a ticket, even if he does not take any animals. Anyone without any animals or with one animal gets a red ticket, anyone with two or three animals gets a green ticket. The green and the red tickets can now 'count' the children and they can be used as representations for the *numbers* of children, in place of the children themselves. For certain purposes we can decide that red and green tickets cancel out. For example, the farmer might decide one day that for some reason the total number of tickets issued must stay at zero, with the convention that red and green tickets in equal numbers are counted as zero. The total number of tickets in the round room will always be zero, yet it is possible to issue a zero number of tickets (i.e. as many red ones as green ones) without everyone being in the round room. For example:

> 3 children with a mouse each, 4 children with a mouse and a guinea pig each, and 1 child with a guinea pig

would have 4 green cards and 4 red cards, yet they would all be in the square room.

If we denote with N, M, H, G, MHG, HG, MG, MH the *numbers* of children with those animals whose first letters are in the appropriate symbols (N = None), then a particular restriction could be written as

$$M+MG+G=0$$

which is a linear restriction on the four-dimensional vector space. Without restrictions, there are four choices available for peopling the square room with children playing with animals; it is possible to choose along the (N, MHG) dimension by choosing a red or a green integer, and similarly it is possible to choose along the dimensions (M, HG), (H, MG) and (G, MH). With the restriction above in force, however, only three such choices may be made; the fourth 'choice' is determined by the stipulated restriction of $M+MG+G=0$. The number of dimensions in a vector space is the number of free choices that are available to determine a vector. By imposing a restriction we have used up a dimension, and are dealing with a three-dimensional vector space.

It would be an obvious step to proceed to the imposition

of a further linear restriction. Assuming the ordinary multiplication table for green and red, i.e.

green times green = green, green times red = red,
red times green = red, red times red = green,

we could impose a further restriction, for example

$$(2 \text{ green}) \times (\text{M, HG}) + (3 \text{ red}) \times (\text{G, MH}) = (\text{N, MHG})$$

where the brackets show the number of green or red counters that are obtained from the dimension indicated.

For instance, N = 5, M = 7, H = 10, G = 3 will satisfy *both* restrictions, the numbers being of course all 'green' numbers. It is clear that MG = 10 red, because H = 10 green. Thus

$$\text{M} + \text{MG} + \text{G} = 7 \text{ green} + 10 \text{ red} + 3 \text{ green} = 0$$

and

$$(2 \text{ green})\ \text{M} + (3 \text{ red})\ \text{G} = (2 \text{ green}).(7 \text{ green}) + (3 \text{ red}).\ (3 \text{ green}) = 14 \text{ green} + 9 \text{ red} = 5 \text{ green}.$$

This second equation gives the required value, since the assigned value of N is 5. It is easily verified that any constant multiple of the vector (5, 7, 10, 3) will also satisfy both conditions. The problem can now be posed whether there are any other solutions. There must be others, as the restricted space cannot have less than two dimensions. Having found such an independent vector, which also satisfies both conditions, it will be interesting to observe that any *other* solution can be obtained as a sum of multiples of the first two independent solutions, the multiples being obtained by multiplying the vectors by either red or green numbers. Another independent solution would, for example, be

N = 5, M = 4, H = 5, G = 1 or (5, 4, 5, 1), all green numbers.

All the vectors in the restricted two-dimensional sub-space determined by the two restrictions may be obtained as

$$A.(5, 7, 10, 3)+B.(5, 4, 5, 1)$$

where A and B may be chosen independently as any green or red numbers. The free choice of the variables A and B indicates the two-dimensionality of the sub-space.

Where children have experienced these relationships between the numbers of dimensions, of restrictions and of free choice, they will begin to ask the questions that lead to retroactive analysis: 'How do we know that there are no other solutions besides those that can be obtained from the first two independent solutions? It is true that so far we have not found any other kinds, but how can we ever be sure that there are none?' This is the kind of enquiry which can lead children on to the study of linear dependence and independence, determinants, etc. But before a proof of any kind is attempted children must feel the need for proof, and they will not feel such a need without the kind of preliminary experience described here. A proof is a chain of class-inclusions, consisting of pieces like 'If property A is true of object x, then property B is also true of object x', which is the same thing as saying 'The class of objects defined by property A is included in the class of objects defined by property B'. Such 'pieces' cannot be appreciated if the constituent classes have not been freely handled, and relevant questions asked about this structure. But once such pieces of reasoning can be appreciated the pieces can be joined into chains, and gradually the idea of proof will emerge. Before a solid conception is established, however, it will be necessary to play about with the constituent pieces of the chains of reasoning, as well as with the chains themselves, ascertaining their properties. For example:

Let the space determined by

$$M+MG+G=0 \text{ and } (2g)M+(2r)G=N$$

be denoted by S. We know that all vectors V in space S are expressible as

$$V = A.(5, 7, 10, 3) + B.(5, 4, 5, 1)$$

where the numbers are all green, i.e. indicate the numbers of children (i) with no animals, (ii) with one mouse, (iii) with one hamster, (iv) with one guinea pig, and A and B are some numbers, possibly red or green.

Suppose we have found that $V_1 = (5, 13, 20, 7)$ (all green numbers) is a vector in space S. From these two facts we *conclude* that there are two numbers A and B such that

$$(5, 13, 20, 7) = A.(5, 7, 10, 3) + B.(5, 4, 5, 1)$$

The 'reasoning' was as follows:

All vectors V in S possess the property A (namely of being expressible in a certain way)
Vector V_1 is in S,

therefore

Vector V_1 has the property A (i.e. V_1 is expressible as a sum of multiples of a certain two special vectors).

This is an elementary piece of reasoning, bringing together in a logical order some of the properties of the mathematical structures and of the 'objects' (vectors in this case) in them. Such pieces can be threaded together, and such chains are what the mathematician calls proofs.

We have already seen that a logical implication is equivalent to a class-inclusion. The calculus of classes or of sets, as they are called in modern mathematics, should clearly form an important part of any mathematical training. Preliminary work with sets can be done with six-year-olds,[1] as long as set variables are avoided. Work on the union, common parts, inclusion, identity and distinctness of sets may be started at any time during children's mathematical training, and such work will repay handsome

[1] See the work carried out in the Palo Alto schools, California, by Suppes, Director of the Mathematical Institute for the Social Sciences, Stanford University.

dividends when they come to questions about reasoning itself. For example:

Property A *implies* Property B

then also

Not possessing property B *implies* Not possessing property A.

In terms of our example:

V obeys the two restrictions defining the space S
implies
V can be expressed as A.(5, 7, 10, 3)+B.(5, 4, 5, 1)

It is perhaps sometimes useful to realize that in this case

V cannot be expressed as A.(5, 7, 10, 3)+B.(5, 4, 5, 1)
implies
V does not obey the two restrictions defining space S, i.e. V is not a vector in space S.

The second implication is known to logicians as the *contraposition* of the first implication. It is surprising how often the contraposition of an implication is confused with the *converse* of the implication, or very often with the contraposition of the converse. The converse of an implication only holds if the corresponding classes or sets are identical, not merely if one set is included in the other. The schematic diagrams below indicate the difference between the cases where the converse is, and is not, true.

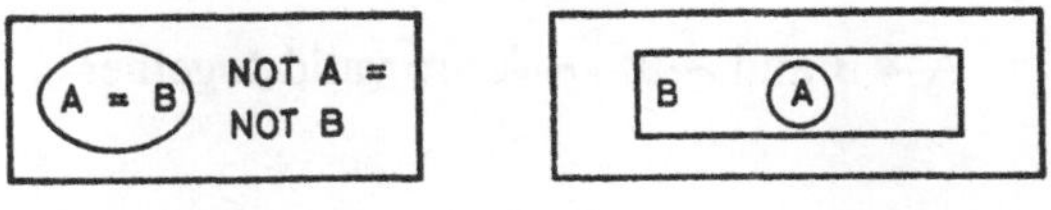

In the first diagram, if object x has property A, it also has property B, but also, *conversely*, if object x has property B, it also has property A. Object x can be imagined inside the circle which is inside the rectangle in the left-hand diagram.

It will be clear that if object y does not have the property A, then it does not have the property B either; if it did, it would be inside the circle and so would have property A. Similarly if object y does not have the property B, it cannot have the property A either. In this case the whole class of objects is neatly divided into two parts, those with the properties A and B, and those without either of these properties. If the objects are triangles, property A could for example be equiangularity, property B equilaterality.

On the second diagram the situation is not quite so neat. Objects with property A are inside the circle, objects with property B are inside the inner rectangle. All relevant objects are inside the outer rectangle. If an object has property A, it also has the property B, but not conversely. If it has the property B, it *may* have the property A, but it may not. This is represented on the diagram by the existence of parts of the inner rectangle which are outside the circle. But what about the contraposition? If an object does not have the property B, then it lies between the two rectangles, i.e. outside the inner one and inside the outer one. It automatically lies outside the circle, and so the object does not have the property A. On the other hand if an object does not have the property A, it could well have the property B for all that, as it could be outside the inner part, the circle, and yet inside the inner rectangle.

Denoting by A the sentence 'an object x has the property A', by B the sentence 'an object x has the property B', by $\sim$A the sentence 'an object does not have the property A', and by $\sim$B the sentence 'an object does not have the property B', it is clear that the implications

$$A \rightarrow B \text{ and } \sim B \rightarrow \sim A \text{ are valid together}$$

and

$$B \rightarrow A \text{ and } \sim A \rightarrow \sim B \text{ are valid together.}$$

If the properties A and B determine coextensive sets of objects in the universe of objects being considered, then all four implications are valid together. The most common mistake is to infer $\sim A \rightarrow \sim B$ from $A \rightarrow B$, which is clearly unjustifiable in the general inclusion situation when the two sets in question are not identical. Such mistakes are so common, even at university level, that it is certain that children's training in logical thinking is deficient somewhere, as the incidence of mistakes in far more complex structures is less frequent. The study of set theory, along with the accompanying logical relations, would undoubtedly go far towards filling the gap in the training that now exists.[1]

How could such a logical situation be illustrated by means of a mathematical story—or perhaps we should call it a logical story? The mouse-hamster-guinea pig farm already provides a prototype. Let us call the two restrictions R_1 and R_2, and the two special vectors in terms of which the restricted sub-space can be expressed V_1 and V_2. Any vector in the sub-space can then be expressed as

$$A.V_1+B.V_2$$

where A and B are red or green numbers (i.e. negative or positive integers, or fractions, if abstraction has already been made from the actual animals, which the children would not like to think of as dismembered!). We have the implications:

$$(V \text{ obeys } R_1 \text{ and } V \text{ obeys } R_2) \rightarrow (V=A.V_1+B.V_2);$$
$$(V=A.V_1+B.V_2) \rightarrow (V \text{ obeys } R_1 \text{ and } V \text{ obeys } R_2)$$

The farmer might say to the children that if a group of children can be found who obey restrictions R_1 and R_2, this group can go and help him feed the animals. Or he could designate the two vectors, i.e. two special groups of children V_1 and V_2, and say that any number of such groups, or opposite groups, can get together and form a gang; but

[1] This is being tried out in Cambridge, Mass., in Hilo, Hawaii, and in Adelaide, Australia, in co-operation with the International Study Group for Mathematics-Learning. Subjects are 5 to 6 year olds and response has been incredibly favourable.

before they can go and help him feed the animals, 'opposite' pairs of children who may have been generated in making up the gang must go back to the round room, and hope for better luck next time. The meaning of these implications, one of which is the converse of the other, is that whichever of these two instructions the farmer gives out for the composition of the feeding gangs, exactly the same gangs will be possible under both instructions. Suppose, for the sake of argument, that he gives out the second set of instructions. The farmer's brother, who works on the farm, is less particular, and announces that he will have any gang that obeys restriction R_1. Now we have the following situation:

Being in the farmer's gang implies that you could have been in the brother's gang.

But it is *NOT TRUE* that

Being in the brother's gang implies that you could have been in the farmer's gang.

Although you might have been in the farmer's gang, too, if your gang by chance also obeyed restriction R_2, this is certainly not *necessarily* so, because the brother was only requiring R_1 to be obeyed by the gang. There is no guarantee that R_2 has been obeyed and, if it has not, you definitely could not have gone to feed the animals with the farmer.

Now what about the contraposition? This would state:

Not being able to be in the brother's gang
implies
Not being able to be in the farmer's gang.

This implication is clearly a true one, because the only reason for a group not to be acceptable as a gang for the brother is that the group does not obey R_1. Since to be acceptable to the farmer the group has to obey both R_1 and R_2, it is clear that this group will not be acceptable to the farmer.

It is likewise *NOT TRUE* that

Not being able to be in the farmer's gang
implies
Not being able to be in the brother's gang

because you might have been excluded from going with the farmer on account of R_2 not being obeyed by the gang you made up, while R_1 was obeyed by it, in which case the brother would be able to use your gang.

These examples are but a small fraction of the logical games that can be played with any given mathematical story. Games could be constructed to lead to the realization of the equivalence of

$$A \rightarrow B \text{ and } \sim A \text{ or } B \text{ (material implication)}$$

or the equivalence of

$$\sim(A \text{ and } B) \text{ is equivalent to } (\sim A) \text{ or } (\sim B) \text{ (De Morgan's rule).}$$

The conscious realization of such methods of reasoning is useful not only in mathematics but in other branches of science and indeed in everyday conversation.

When children have played about with implications and have learned the meanings of such terms as converse and contraposition, the relationship between the implications

$$A \rightarrow B,\ B \rightarrow A,\ \sim B \rightarrow \sim A, \text{ and } \rightarrow \sim A \rightarrow \sim B$$

may be connected to the mathematical group with four elements which was introduced in the last chapter in the shape of a card-game and the half-turns about three mutually perpendicular axes. The four implications can be the 'states' in the game, the operators being as follows:

(I) Identity operator, leaves state unchanged
(CP) Contraposition operator
(CN) Converse operator
(N) Operator which places negations in front of each member of the implication.

It must be agreed that a double negation reduces to an affirmation, i.e. that $\sim\sim A$ is the same as A, so that

$$N(\sim A \rightarrow \sim B) = (A \rightarrow B)$$

and similarly for others. It is easily verified that each operator, when performed twice, will restore the original state. Such a double operation, in fact, is always equivalent to the identity operator. Any two of the three operators (CP), (CN), and (N), when performed one after the other, will have the same effect as the third one. We therefore have the table[1]:

	I	N	CP	CN
I	I	N	CP	CN
N	N	I	CN	CP
CP	CP	CN	I	N
CN	CN	CP	N	I

which the reader may compare with the tables obtained for the 4-element groups in the last chapter. We have travelled far from the dancing and boating children with whom we began. Yet what has been described is only a small beginning compared with what could be done. The power to manipulate our imagery is there in every one of us, and the skill develops with practice. It would be a great pity not to make image-manipulation one of the teacher's allies in helping children to become eager to learn mathematical structures.

[1] Piaget has used this table in his accounts of children's logic

5

The Power of Mathematical Symbolism

MATHEMATICS is a language specially adapted to the expression and communication of particular types of information. Like other languages, it is capable of organic growth, a growth which is stimulated by the discovery of new connections and relationships and the need for new mathematical symbols. Particularly over the past hundred years or so, the language of mathematics has become so rich that not even mathematicians can possibly be familiar with all of it. The man in the street has been left sadly behind, and a layman listening to two mathematicians discussing an intricate problem might as well be listening to a foreign language, for all the information that he receives. A dangerous rift has developed between those 'in the know' and the very men for whose eventual benefit the developing mathematics is being discovered.

Those of us who are (i) quickly aware of new structures, and (ii) able to store information in symbolic form, are the ones liable to become mathematicians. It is possible, as we have seen, to increase the number of people who are sensitive to structure in the environment. But mathematical and other scientific structures are growing so complex that the problem of symbolically storing the information gained is becoming crucial. It is still an open question whether our scarcity of mathematicians is due to the scarcity of people who can apprehend structures, or of people who can store such structures in symbolized forms. The reason is that only the few people who apprehend ever get the chance of symbolizing. If it now turns out to be possible to familiarize the majority of people with mathematical structures through experiences such as have been described here and elsewhere, we may find that the symbolic manipulation is the less difficult part of the business. At present most people find mathematical manipulations difficult to learn, because on the whole they do not know what it is they are really manipulating.

The apprehension of structures and the symbolization process are not altogether distinct, and in fact there is reason to believe that each acts as a stimulus on the other. Although it is true that we cannot meaningfully talk about something, i.e. symbolize it, until we have learnt by experience what it is we are talking about, the fact that we grow up in a social environment cannot be ignored. In this environment *other people* talk about things that we do not understand. The whole process of learning our mother-tongue is one of sorting out our experiences vis-à-vis our environment and putting them in correspondence with the initially meaningless chatter that we hear all about us. Abstract words representing quite complex situations are often learnt only in adult life, through evaluating what is common to the contexts in which the words occur. All of us undergo this process all our lives, and it is mostly beneath the level of consciousness that the sorting out occurs. I have heard, however, of the case of one person with a phenomenal visual memory who learnt English by picking up a book and starting to read it. After having read more than half the book, without any previous knowledge of English and without having once used a dictionary, her husband expressed his incredulity. He decided to test her. She was able to give a full account of what she had read; what is more, upon being asked what a certain word meant, she thought for a moment and said: 'That word occurred on page 97 near the top in such and such a context, and it further occurred in three more places in a number of other contexts. It follows that the word means something like this'—and she gave a very near definition of the meaning. I have already remarked how quickly children learn a foreign language if they are placed in an environment where the language is spoken. The symbols are picked out of the general chorus of noise and associated with the relevant situations. The Direct Method of teaching languages is based on the provision of situations, systematically graded, in which associations with situations and with contexts go side by side to fix the 'meanings' of the sentences in the foreign language.

Unfortunately the parallel between language-learning and mathematics-learning breaks down in one very important particular. We do not grow up within earshot of unintelligible mathematical noises, in the same way as we grow up hearing the noises of our mother-tongue. Even if we have a reasonably complete diet of mathematical experiences through the use of structured materials, mathematical games and the like, the mathematical chatter will still be lacking. In consequence, a certain amount of artificiality will have to enter into our introduction of mathematical symbolism. Now there is evidence that children engaged in manipulating mathematical imagery or structured materials evolve their own kind of rudimentary symbolism. A rigorist attitude on the part of the teacher can in such cases retard or altogether stop learning. For example, the notations $y=x^2$ and $f(x)=x^2$ are not necessarily the best symbols to express the nascent idea of function; something like $x \rightarrow x^2$ might suit the situation better. It certainly gives visual expression to the correspondence between x and x^2, even indicating the direction of this correspondence.

To help in smoothing out difficulties for children completing the symbolization process, intermediate stages may be necessary. Just as the earliest writing was picture writing, so the first mathematical writing might well be a reproduction of pictorial imagery. When vectors are introduced by means of concrete objects such as squares, circles, square frames and circular frames, the notation could at first consist of actually drawing the objects.

would denote 2 circular frames and 3 squares. A further stage would bring in the use of natural numbers, when the same vector would be written

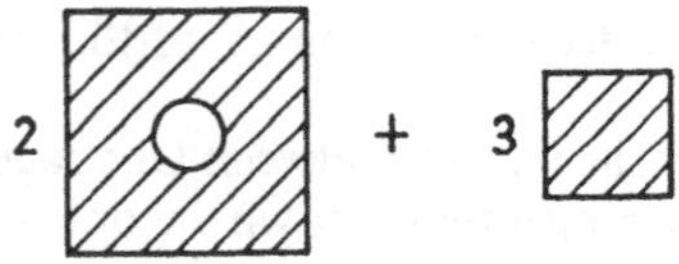

This stage could be followed by verbal abbreviations such as

$$2cf+3s$$

and by the introduction of directed numbers such as twiddle and bar numbers or green and red numbers, i.e.

$$\bar{2}c+\tilde{3}s$$

As the variation of experiences progressively enriches the mathematical environment, even these symbols can be replaced by

$$\bar{2}e_1+\tilde{3}e_2$$

where e_1 and e_2 denote already abstracted 'unit vectors' in the two-dimensional vector space. In other words, the unit vectors could be imagined as boys, girls, men and women, children with animals, arrows pointing in various directions, coloured counters, or any system of objects with the required properties. It should be noted, however, that the final image will not be a composite of all the image-formation or image-manipulation situations; it will be some grey phantom-like image which is endowed with the relevant properties attributed to the structure.

Alternative series of symbols could naturally be thought of, and in any particular situation teachers will no doubt be guided by responses from the class during class or group discussion on 'how shall we write this down?' It might be objected that the plus sign is premature in the notation

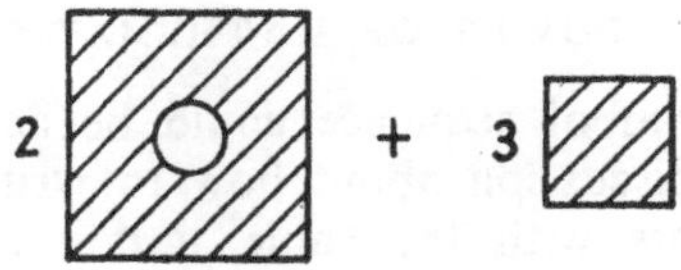

because addition has not been explicitly introduced. Teachers will have to decide for themselves whether to be guided by such logical subtleties or not. An alternative series of symbols which meets this objection would be:

$$(2\boxed{\circ}, 3\square), (2cf, 3s), (2\bar{c}, 3\tilde{s}), (2c, 3s), (\bar{2}, \tilde{3});$$

where either the third or the fourth member of the series could be omitted. The use of both might cause confusion if it has not been suggested by the children.

Addition could now be introduced, starting with something obvious like

$$(\bar{2}, 0)+(0, \tilde{3})=(\bar{2}, \tilde{3})$$

One must remember, however, that the process of learning is a psychological, not a logical process, and a logically tidy sequence will not necessarily provide the best method of learning an abstract structure. In point of fact, a carefully graded sequence of symbols is not called for in every case. There are even dangers in structuring the symbolism so as to associate it too closely with certain experiences. If such symbolism is used, it is wise to use also other sets of symbols which come close to depicting other sets of experiences. In other words, the variability principle might be used during the formative stage of the symbolization process. For example, arrows drawn on cardboard pieces can be used to represent a two-dimensional space, and the vectors can be depicted by the drawing of these arrows. Squares and square frames could correspond to ↑ and ↓, circles and circular frames to → and ←. In this case the vector we are considering would be written as

$$\leftarrow \leftarrow \uparrow \uparrow \uparrow$$

and another symbol sequence could be developed from there. Group discussion about how to write down both kinds of vectors with the same notation could easily lead, with a little additional guidance, to a viable vector notation.

Just as making the symbols resemble the experiences too closely has its dangers, so has making the experiences too close to the conventional symbols. Vectors are usually represented by arrows leading from one point to another in diagrams, and it would be tempting to use exclusively spatial experiences to lead children to the idea of a vector. The steps taken in two perpendicular directions from the centre of the classroom are certainly a good starting point. Unless, however, other experiences of a non-spatial character accompany the 'stepping' experiences, the concept of vector developed by the children will inevitably be tied to that of spatial displacement; that is, to three dimensions or less. There is nothing in the mathematical concept of a vector which has anything essentially to do with space. A vector is a set of independent variables, the components.[1] These may be anything measurable and could be extremely numerous. This is one of the reasons why vectors should be introduced by the manipulation of concrete objects or of images. The same argument applies to any other mathematical structure or process; the differential coefficient should not be regarded as *only* the slope of a curve, nor the integral as *only* the area under a curve. If care is taken to vary the mathematical situations the symbols will denote the pure mathematical structures, stripped of irrelevant spatial and other trimmings. A greater measure of abstraction is achieved out of a richer variety of experiences. If one of the functions of symbolism is to fixate the structure learnt and render it permanently available, then the symbolism must only do this when a mathematically desirable degree of abstraction of the symbolized structure has been achieved. The most likely reason for the general ossification of

[1] Or it is a set of objects of thought satisfying certain axioms, if one tends to be axiomatically minded

mathematics in children's minds at an early stage is the rash use of symbols, i.e. *the introduction and manipulation of symbolism before adequate experience has been enjoyed of that which is symbolized.*

The passing from the experiential, pre-symbolic stage to the symbolic stage can be facilitated through the use of a graded series of symbols, starting with a near-pictorial reproduction of what is symbolized, and ending with the conventional mathematical symbolism in current use. This means that we begin by using symbols as another, rather close embodiment of the mathematical experience. On the other hand it is also possible to use embodiments as symbols. The green and red counters representing the basis-algebra of positive and negative integers are an example of this kind of symbolic embodiment, and likewise the green and red tickets that the farmer gives to the children who play with the animals. When we say that there are children in the square room with a total of 3 red tickets, equal numbers of red and green tickets not counting, we have endowed these tickets with the properties of positive and negative integers. The tickets are acting as symbols in exactly the same way as $+1$, -1, $+2$, -2, $+3$, -3, . . . act as symbols. We can use a series of such embodiment-symbols, starting with full embodiment, and proceeding to more and more conventionalized embodiments, until the completely conventional written symbols are reached.

The Cuisenaire rods use this principle. At first, the rods do actually represent amounts in terms of cubic centimetres (the units not being necessarily the centimetre cubes). When they are crossed to 'represent' a product, they remind the learner of the rectangle, which was the full representation of the product, but is now not being fully used. Subsequently towers of rods will represent powers, until eventually the rods are discarded and the conventional mathematical symbols are used. In such cases great care must be taken that the symbolism does not become tied to the manipulation of the rods but rather to the mathematical structure symbolized by the manipulation of the rods. This is best achieved, as we know, by varying the embodiment, that is, by extending the scope of the children's experiences through the physical manipulation of other objects, or by image-manipulation.

In considering the use of symbols, we have to remember that mathematical thinking contains as constituent parts, among other processes, those of abstraction and generalization.[1] When an abstraction is achieved, the learner classifies a great number of situations as a certain type. A symbol is required to fixate the new abstraction, which is a creation not previously present in the learner's mind. A new word is therefore necessary, to enable the new creation to be talked about. Symbols are thus abstract to the extent that they symbolize an abstract creation; but they are clearly not abstract in themselves because, divorced from the meaning just given to them, they are mere signs with no particular relevance. In the same way, when a generalization is achieved, a symbol is required to fixate the realization of the extent to which a certain structure will reach. We may say that abstraction is the intensive, generalization the extensive, facet of mathematical thinking. Often the same symbolism is used for both these facets. A simple case in point is the notion of a square number. When we write x^2, we mean something which is both abstract and general. Any kind of situation in which objects (real or idealized) are grouped into as many groups as the number of objects in each group is described by the symbol x^2, where the symbol x represents the number of such groups (or of objects per group). Writing x^2 also implies a degree of generality extending at least to an initial section of the natural numbers, but most likely to all natural numbers. This generality could extend by degrees to rational, then to real numbers. But already at the stage of squaring natural numbers, the *same symbol* x^2 symbolizes both the abstraction and the generalization that must take place before the symbol can become mathematically operational.

[1] Z. P. Dienes, 'On abstraction and generalization' *Harvard Educational Review* Summer, 1961

Sometimes breadth of abstraction and degree of generality are allowed to proceed at different rates. If a generalization or a series of generalizations is made on a narrow front, i.e. without an adequate breadth of abstraction, it may well be found that symbolization is resisted. This tends to happen in a scholastic situation where there is great pressure to 'cover the ground'. Examples were recorded during the 1960–1 Mathematics-Learning Project at Harvard where one subject appeared to predict absolutely accurately in situations equivalent to the formula $(x+2)^2=x^2+4x+4$, yet strenuously resisted the notation x times x (i.e. not even x^2). On the other hand, he accepted 4 times x without difficulty. He had only had experience of the corresponding mathematical situations in one embodiment (small wooden squares). Presumably he had not experienced 'as many rows as there are small squares in a row' as a member of the class 'as many groups as there are things in a group', whereas '4 groups of so many things' must have been met with in a great many situations. Consequently 4 times x was sufficiently abstract to be symbolized, but not x times x. It is usually difficult to obtain reliable experimental evidence of this, as school children are under pressure to perform. On the whole, they will accept anything as long as they are told that it is 'the right answer'. The children in the experimental group were in a reasonably free situation, and had become accustomed to the permissive atmosphere of the experimental sessions. This particular child was at any rate free enough to object, and made his objection quite plain!

It is very easy to be under the impression that children are getting on beautifully, when the reason for their invariably correct response is that the mathematical structure is being embodied in a single type of situation. Varying the embodiment will often block the response. So, too, will varying the way in which the questions are asked. One particular form of questioning may draw the children's attention to a particular perceptual aspect of the material which happens to be the one that they have singled out as their aid in solving the problems. For example, in the study of fractional indices described in the second chapter, extraction of roots and raising to powers may be very closely tied to manipulation of the 'position-values' of the series of blocks. Taking the series to the base 5, one might point at the block with 125 units and require a child to raise it to the $\frac{2}{3}$ power. The correct solution, i.e., selecting the block with 25 units, can be achieved by taking the block $\frac{2}{3}$ of the way up from the zero position to the 125-block. This is a purely perceptual association with a property of the blocks when set out in a series. The question 'How do you get from the 125-block to the 25-block by taking roots and raising powers?' might leave the child in confusion. Even when he has worked out that it is possible to take the cube-root, i.e. go down to the 5-block, and then raise this to the second power, or else go up to the next cube, and then take the cube-root of that cube, it is not at all certain that he will associate this activity with taking the $\frac{2}{3}$ power of 125. The symbol

$$125^{\frac{2}{3}}$$

should not be allowed to attach itself to a particular perceptual detail of the mathematical situations that are being used to help the child. To provide the symbolism before the structure is genuinely learnt is to invite trouble.

What are the signs, then, of a sufficient degree of abstraction and of generality attained to enable children to accept confidently the appropriate symbolism? Too little research has been done in this field to allow any confident statements. There are, however, some indications. When two or more embodiments are being used with the intention of broadening the basis of a structure, a child may say: 'We don't really need all these. They are really doing the same thing. Why not have just one?' This is a suggestion that one of the situations be used as a prototype of the others, i.e. that one embodiment be used as a set of symbols. The road to written symbols is then not difficult to travel.

Attempts at generalizing are often indicated by children

saying that they are trying to find 'the pattern'. Once the pattern is found the road is open to its description, at first in full or shortened sentences, but eventually in the shorthand of conventional symbolism. An act of generalization, or of suspected generalization, is often accompanied by the use of the word 'always', as in 'you always go up two', or 'it's always three times as much', or the like. It may be necessary to guard children, particularly bright children, against hasty generalizations. 'The pattern' may turn out to be the wrong one, and some time may have to be spent in studying examples of plausible but untrue generalizations. The ideal is for every child to arrive at his own generalizations, but this is manifestly impossible owing to the size of classes and the limitations of time. Teachers should, however, make reasonably sure that every child does *some* generalizing on his own. This can then be followed by the necessary formulations, and the trimming of these formulations, leading finally to the development of appropriate symbolism.

The value of symbols is that they make all the information contained in a structure readily available at a moment's notice. But why do we want such information to be so readily available? Most likely, it is so as to be able to process this information and arrive at fresh information. The symbolism in this case acts as an embodiment of the structure or structures; it is manipulated at random or in more or less purposeful ways, and through such manipulations the additional information is obtained. This fresh information in turn allows us to make predictions in real or imagined situations.

Consider the change-over problem in the dance situation, formulated as follows:

'There is a certain unknown number of people waiting in the refreshment room. The identical twins of these people as well as 4 more boys announce that a change must take place. After the change, when all the couples have gone dancing, there are 13 girls left in the refreshment room. How many people were there in the refreshment room before the change, and how many of these were boys, girls, men or women?'

This type of situation, along with others isomorphic to the type, has been symbolized by the notation of complex numbers. Boys are denoted by $+1$, girls by -1, men by $+i$, and women by $-i$. This symbolization enables us to concentrate the whole power of the complex algebra on this problem. The symbolized form of the problem will be

$$Y.(Y+4)=-13$$

which we can turn into the equivalent statement

$$(Y+2)^2=-9$$

i.e. into the disjunctive assertion

either $Y+2=3i$ *or* $Y+2=-3i$

therefore

either $Y=-2+3i$ *or* $Y=-2-3i$

All this manipulation takes place without our paying the slightest attention to boys, girls, men or women. We have fed the problem into a machine, with the properties of which we are well familiar, and now the machine can do the work for us. We turn the handle of the machine, i.e. manipulate the symbols, and the problem is solved. We can make the following statement about the population of the refreshment room:

'Before the change-over there must have been
either
2 girls and 3 men
or
2 girls and 3 women in the refreshment room.'

What is it which makes the symbol-system such a powerful weapon that with its aid we can obtain a systematic solution to a somewhat intricate problem? *First*, there is an exact one-to-one correspondence between the elements of the imagined situation and the elements of the mathematical structure called into play. *Second*, we are able to run back and forth at will between the corresponding elements of the imagined situation and the structure. The correspondence must hold exactly *both ways*, because at the beginning we have to translate the situation into the language of the structure, and at the end we have to translate the language of the structure back again into the language of the situation. To be able to pick out the relevant structure which will do the trick for any particular situation is no mean achievement, and this is where the breadth of abstraction of the structure learnt is important. If we have encountered the same structure in many different situations, we get the feel of it, and somehow recognize the feel of it when we encounter it again, even if disguised in quite unfamiliar situations. This will help us not only in picking the right structure for the solution of the problem, but also in the two translation jobs that form part of the process. If we have played about with the structure, become familiar with its rules, and learnt to play along with it by its rules, we shall find no difficulty in manipulating the symbolism into the form which will yield a solution to our problem.

In the conventional method of learning mathematics a great deal of attention is devoted to symbol-manipulations, sometimes of an extremely intricate character. It is seldom that such manipulation-learning forms part of a larger and more purposeful pattern. The all too common result is that certain manipulations of signs (which we can hardly call symbols, as they tend to get more and more meaningless) are learnt as patterns for answering the types of questions which habitually occur in examinations. Factorizing of quadratic functions is brought to a fine art by most students of mathematics, yet these same students almost invariably find it beyond them to solve the tank-problem of the first chapter, in spite of the fact that it is a clear-cut situation in which the factorization of

$$x^2 - x - 6$$

leads to the solution of the problem. Some children, in fact, look around for ways of setting up simultaneous equations, since they *know* that this is the drill whenever two unknowns are to be determined. 'Knowing' resulting from drill-teaching only means the establishment of stimulus-response patterns, and it is easy to show up such 'knowledge' for what it is worth. Any mathematics teacher knows that it would be possible to fail the whole class, with perhaps one or two brilliant exceptions, merely by putting unusual examples in the examination paper. If mathematics has been learnt as a system of structures fitting into one another, it is impossible to trip students up in this way, because they recognize the situations in which the structures are relevant.

In the average mathematical-learning situation the thread between reality and the manipulation of 'symbols' is very thin, if not definitely severed. Even in situations based on concrete mathematical experiences, this thread may break. Either the teacher or the student becomes over-enthusiastic about the *formal* properties of the rule-structures being unravelled through mathematical experiences, and loses touch with reality. Constant feedback, or at least opportunity of feedback, into concrete situations from which the structures have been abstracted will guard against this danger. Particularly if a formal generalization has been made, within a certain formal mathematical framework (as, for example, generalization to fractional from integral indices), children should immediately be tested on their ability to apply the new general structure to concrete situations.

The most exciting aspect of symbols for the mathematician is their creative function. By enabling him to store an enormous amount of information compactly, symbols give him the sort of material that paints provide for the painter or stone for the sculptor. Through their judicious manipulation he can ask exciting questions, as well as solve problems that other people have not been able to solve. He can transform problems to equivalent problems, or pass from one problem to allied problems which may appear more interesting. In other words, there is an art in the handling of symbols. Children are given paints with which to obtain first-hand experience in the art of painting, they are given plasticene with which to make models, they are even encouraged in more enlightened schools to write poems and plays; but where are children given the opportunity to have first-hand experience in the art of mathematics? There was a child, the only one in the experimental groups in the Harvard Mathematics-Learning Project, who positively used mathematical symbolism in a creative way, transforming one problem into another problem. For full verbatim reports the reader must be referred to my book describing the experiments,[1] but a short report is given below to show what an eight-year-old boy can do.

The problem set was this:

'Suppose you have (Y+4) groups of Y things in each group. How many more things would you have to have before you were sure that you could arrange your things into just as many groups as there are things in each group?

Write down the solution of the problem in the language of algebra.

Try to explain what you have done on the balance.'

The 'balance' was a beam which could turn freely about its midpoint in a vertical plane, with nine hooks fixed at regular intervals on either side of the fulcrum. The hook nearest the fulcrum was at the same distance from the fulcrum as the contiguous hooks were from each other. Metal washers of equal weights were available for hanging on the hooks. The hooks were numbered from the fulcrum outwards by means of figures printed on the beam.

The boy was already familiar with the idea of multiple embodiment and could translate problems freely from one embodiment to another. In this case, however, the problem was so formulated that any embodiment could be used or none. The piece about the balance was put in as a matter of routine, to ascertain that he was capable of feeding back

[1] *An experimental study of mathematics-learning* Hutchinson, London, 1963

any new discoveries into some physical situation. He was also quite at home with the use of letters meaning any number that he or anyone else might choose.

The subject began to attack the problem symbolically from the start. He arrived at a few exemplars of perfect squares, which he did not check particularly carefully (i.e. by giving Y several values). He was also not working on a minimal problem; that is to say, any number when added, as long as it made a perfect square, would do. He several times looked over what he had written, as though trying to gather inspiration from the formalism. He noticed that if $Y=1$, then it happened that

$$(Y+4)Y+20=25=(Y+4)^2$$

and the occurrence of the $(Y+4)$ on both sides of the equation intrigued him. He began to wonder how this could be achieved with other values of Y, and arrived at

$$(Y+4)Y+24=6^2=(Y+4)^2 \text{ for } Y=2$$

He was quite sure that the same feat could be achieved for any value of Y. The session ended at this point.

Without very consciously realizing it, the subject had transformed the problem

'What is Z if $Y.(Y+4)+Z$ is always equal to some square for *all* values of Y?'

into

'What is the value of Z, given the value of Y, to make $Y.(Y+4)+Z=(Y+4)^2$ true?'

In other words he transformed an identity problem into a function problem, the turning point being that he was intrigued by something that emerged in the formalism. The two problems were eventually separately formalized and solved, and the difference between them consciously appreciated.

The activity of this small boy might seem somewhat trivial. But it is not the mathematical content that is important, but the use he made of the symbolism. This use was creative in the sense that he created a new problem for himself.

We do not need long to realize that it cannot be the symbols in isolation which have a creative role; it must be the symbols together with whatever they symbolize. When a mathematician makes use of symbols in a creative way, he manipulates the structures in his mind just as much as the symbols on the paper, for without the structures the symbols would be meaningless signs. In other words, however 'formal' a mathematician may think he is, when he thinks creatively, he does actually put things together to see what they look like, or perhaps feel like (depending on whether he is a visual or tactile image-manipulator).

Let us take an example from vector spaces. Supposing that the parallelism between sets of steps and sets of certain types of objects, and sets of changes in the values of certain variables, is established. Supposing then that it is desired to introduce what mathematicians call a 'metric' into the vector space; that is, some function of a vector which can be described as its 'length'. The theorem of Pythagoras will lead to an easy solution in the case of the steps, in which case the 'length' of the vector corresponds to the meaning given to the word 'length' in everyday life. Even in three dimensions, provided the unit vectors in all directions have the same 'length', the expression

$$(x_1^2+x_2^2+x_3^2)^{\frac{1}{2}}$$

still attributes to the vector (x_1, x_2, x_3) a 'length' which has the everyday meaning. This 'meaning' could be transferred lock, stock and barrel to other representations of vectors, such as squares, triangles and circles, with their opposites square frames, triangle frames and circle frames. For example, the 'length' of the vector

 or of $(\tilde{2}, \tilde{2}, \bar{1})$

(depending on the stage of symbolization we have reached) would be $\tilde{3}$. This is because $(\tilde{2}^2+\tilde{2}^2+\tilde{1}^2)=\tilde{9}$, and the 'positive' or 'twiddle' square root of $\tilde{9}$ is $\tilde{3}$—or in another context, 3 green counters or tickets.

Now what should be the 'length' of a four- or five- or n-dimensional vector? This is where the symbolism assumes its creative role. The 'length' of (x_1, x_2) is $(x_1^2+x_2^2)^{\frac{1}{2}}$, the 'length' of (x_1, x_2, x_3) is $(x_1^2+x_2^2+x_3^2)^{\frac{1}{2}}$, so why not define the 'length' of $(x_1, x_2, \ldots x_n)$ as

$$(x_1^2+x_2^2+\ \ldots\ +x_2^n)^{\frac{1}{2}}\ ?$$

Similarly the cosine of the angle between the vectors

$$(x_1, x_2, x_3) \text{ and } (y_1, y_2, y_3) \text{ is}$$

$$\frac{x_1y_1+x_2y_2+x_3y_3}{(\text{length of X}).(\text{length of Y})}$$

so why not define the cosine of the angle between $X=(x_1, x_2, \ldots x_n)$ and $Y=(y_1, y_2, \ldots y_n)$ as

$$\frac{x_1y_1+x_2y_2+\ \ldots\ +x_ny_n}{(\text{length of X}).(\text{length of Y})}\ ?$$

When we do this we formally extend the definitions of length and angle to n-dimensional spaces. The symbols have become in some sense autonomous, freed from the shackles of concrete images. On the other hand, would an angle between two n-dimensional vectors *mean* anything to us if we had not established a close connection between the geometrical situation and the symbolism on the one hand, and between the geometrical situation and the more abstract mathematical situation of a vector space on the other? Have we not thereby achieved this phantom-like image of a many-dimensional space, which has the *formal* properties that our space would have if in fact it had more than three dimensions?

Once the number of dimensions has been divorced from its purely spatial connections, we can, for fun, reintroduce spatial terms into our conversations about the properties of n-dimensional vector spaces. Let us see what was happening in the farm story of the last chapter, expressed in fully symbolic form. The restrictions R_1 and R_2 can be written down as the equations:

$$(R_1) \qquad \tilde{1}.x_2+\bar{1}.x_3+\tilde{1}.x_4=0$$

$$(R_2) \qquad \tilde{2}.x_2+ \qquad \bar{3}.x_4=\tilde{1}.x_1$$

or more conventionally

$$x_2-x_3+x_4=0$$

$$2x_2- \qquad 3x_4=x_1$$

These are the restrictions that must be satisfied by the vector (x_1, x_2, x_3, x_4) to be in the sub-space S. In the story they would be the restrictions imposed by the farmer on groups of children that he would take to feed the animals on the farm. We have two choices for a vector in this sub-space, namely the values of A and B; and

$$A.(5, 7, 10, 3)+B.(5, 4, 5, 1)$$

will certainly be a vector in this sub-space. This is a two-dimensional vector space, and the vectors in it can be denoted by the symbol (A, B) where A and B are to be freely chosen. We also saw that vectors obeying only one or the other of the restrictions R_1 or R_2 form three-dimensional sub-spaces, so that the equations corresponding to these restrictions define a three-dimensional sub-space within the whole four-dimensional space. Vectors obeying *both* the restrictions are to be found in a two-dimensional sub-space, which can be described as the *intersection* of the three-dimensional spaces corresponding to R_1 and to R_2. So two spaces meet in a plane, just as two planes meet in a line and two lines meet in a point. Here we are using the language of geometry, which is a system of symbols expressing relationships between structures, and we are allowing the language to 'run away with itself'; we talk about intersections of spaces, having carried along with us some remnant of the imagery of three-dimensional space, together with the connections of this imagery with the developing structure of the constituent parts of this space. We have truly created something out of almost nothing, even if the image on which we build is so faint that we hardly recognize that it exists. None the less, it does exist, and remains our only link with reality, apparently receding so fast that we might be fearful of losing touch with it altogether. The creative process is always very elusive. But it will be the task of the future teacher of mathematics to put children into carefully selected situations in which their creative urges can be set free, so that they become masters and not slaves of mathematical symbolism.

6

The Power of Mathematical Reasoning

HOWEVER abstract we may imagine we are being about a certain mathematical structure, it is likely that we could be even more abstract. In other words, there may still be irrelevancies which we consider essential parts of the structure but which turn out to be just as irrelevant as the colour or shape of the objects in a collection, when all we are interested in is the number of such objects. In this chapter I shall try to show how the last ounces of irrelevancy can be squeezed out of our mathematical thinking, by the use of a symbolism. Through a minute examination of our symbolic work we should become aware of the purity of the structures we have abstracted from experience or from the manipulation of other structures. We may then begin to speak about 'any structure with such and such properties'. To be able to do this, we must be extremely clear about the interconnection of these properties.

During the construction of some of the algebraic structures we learn at school, we become aware of relationships between variables which are true for all values of the variables. Such relationships are commonly referred to as identities. Let us make a short list of some such identities. (Letters indicate positive or negative integers, and the bar indicates the additive inverse of a number; that is, a has the same absolute value as $\bar{a}$ but the opposite sign.)

We know that all the following are true:

(1) For any number a, b, c, $(a+b)+c=a+(b+c)$.

(2) There is a number, usually denoted by 0, such that for every number a we have $a+0=a=0+a$.

(3) To every pair of numbers a, b, corresponds a number c such that $a+b=c$.

(4) For every number a, there is a number b, such that $a+b=0=b+a$. We shall denote such a number by the symbol $\bar{a}$.

(5) For every pair of numbers a, b, we have $a+b=b+a$.

(6) For any number a, b, and c, $(a.b).c=a.(b.c)$.

(7) For any numbers a, b, c, $(a+b).c=a.c+b.c$.

(8) For any numbers a, b, c, $a.(b+c)=a.b+a.c$.

(9) For any number a, $a.0=0$, and $0.a=0$.

(10) For any pair of numbers a, b, we have the following: $\bar{a}.b=a.\bar{b}$, $a.\bar{b}=\overline{a.b}$, $\bar{a}.\bar{b}=a.b$.

This is still a very short list; if a class of children familiar with the workings of algebraic symbols were asked to add to it, a much longer list would emerge. The problem is now to shorten such a list. Is it possible that some of the items are superfluous, in the sense that they could be *deduced* from some of the other items?[1] Let us try to deduce items (9) and (10) from some of the previous ones. As we do so, we can make notes of the kinds of deductions we are using, and subsequently incorporate these as our rules of procedure. We can substitute 0 for a in (2), and obtain

$$0+0=0; \quad \cdots \quad (\alpha)$$

We can substitute 0 for b and for c in (8), and obtain

$$a.(0+0)=a.0+a.0 \quad \cdots \quad (\beta)$$

We can multiply (α) on both sides of the left by a, and obtain

$$a.(0+0)=a.0 \quad \cdots \quad (\gamma)$$

From the principle ($X=Z$ and $Y=Z \rightarrow X=Y$) we obtain from (β) and (γ) that

$$a.0+a.0=a.0 \quad \cdots \quad (\delta)$$

[1] This idea is due to Robert Davis, Director of the Madison Project, Syracuse University, N.Y., U.S.A.

We can add to (δ) on the right on both sides $\overline{a.o}$, and obtain

$$(a.o+a.o)+\overline{a.o}=a.o+\overline{a.o} \quad \ldots \quad (\epsilon)$$

Substituting in (1) a.o for a, a.o for b and $\overline{a.o}$ for c, we obtain

$$(a.o+a.o)+\overline{a.o}=a.o+(a.o+\overline{a.o}) \quad \ldots \quad (\lambda)$$

and substituting in (4) a.o for a and $\overline{a.o}$ for b, we have

$$a.o+\overline{a.o}=o \quad \ldots \quad (\lambda^+)$$

We can then replace $(a.o+\overline{a.o})$ in (λ) by o and obtain

$$(a.o+a.o)+\overline{a.o}=a.o+o \quad \ldots \quad (\lambda')$$

but substituting a.o for a in (2) we obtain

$$a.o+o=a.o \quad \ldots \quad (\lambda'')$$

then from (ϵ), (λ^+), (λ') and (λ'') and from the transitive property of equality, we have

$$a.o=o$$

Similarly, using (7) instead of (8), we can 'prove' that o.a=o.

Assuming we accept all the ways in which we have linked each of these statements to previous ones, we may consider (9) a superfluous statement on the list.

Let us now try to make a list of the methods of linkage we have employed in arriving at our end-formulae of a.o=o and o.a=o.

We have made use of the following:

(A) Substitution of any particular values in statements which are true for all values of the variables involved.

(B) If x = y has been established by the rules, then in any other established formula x and y are freely interchangeable.
(C) If a = b then also b = a.
(D) If a = b and if b = c then also a = c.
(E) If a = b then also a + x = b + x, as well as a.x = b.x, as well as x.a = x.b.

Let us re-examine which of these rules were used at the various stages of our 'proof'.

(2) to (α), (A); (8) to (β), (A); (α) to (γ), (E); (β) and (γ) to (δ), (C) and (D); (δ) to (ϵ), (E); (1) to (λ), (A); (4) to (λ^+), (A); (λ) and (λ^+) to (λ'), (B); (2) to (λ''), (A); (ϵ) and (λ^+) and (λ') and (λ'') to a.o = o, (C) and (D).

The schema of the proof could be set out in a spatial representation as follows:

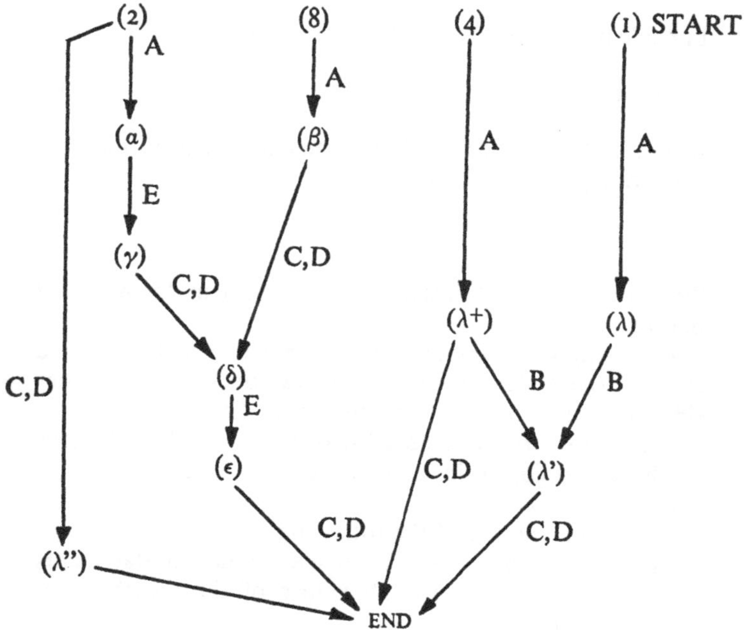

It should perhaps be pointed out that (3) is being used tacitly all the time, as this requirement makes it certain that 'addition' can be carried out. Rules (A) to (E) might themselves be considered redundant; that is, some of these rules could perhaps be 'deduced' from the others. But to determine the validity of this objection, we need to clarify exactly what we mean by 'deduce', when it is a question of deducing methods of deduction from one another. Logical axioms would be necessary to clarify the position, and these would again need their own rules for the deduction of logical statements. It is possible to do this, but the necessary propositional and predicate calculi are beyond the scope of this book.[1] For example the implication

$$(a=b)\rightarrow(b=a)$$

can be deduced from the two 'axioms'

$$\text{(i) } a=a,$$
$$\text{(ii) } a=b\rightarrow(a=c\rightarrow b=c)$$

by means of the axioms and rules of procedure of the propositional calculus, and so rule (C) would become superfluous if the rules were suitably reorganized.

Let us now try to deduce the statements in (10) from the statements (1) to (8); we already know that (9) can be left out of the list. We shall show that (10) can likewise be left out. The schema of the proof would look something like the diagram on page 158.

In this way the whole of (10) may be deduced from statements (1) to (7), making use of no further methods of deduction than were used in the deduction of (9).

The very look of these formal schemes would be enough to frighten some people off the mathematical analysis of structures. They might well ask what was the point of such an analysis. But then what is the point of any kind of

[1] See D. Hilbert and P. Bernays, *Grundlagen der Mathematik* Springer Verlag, Berlin, 1934

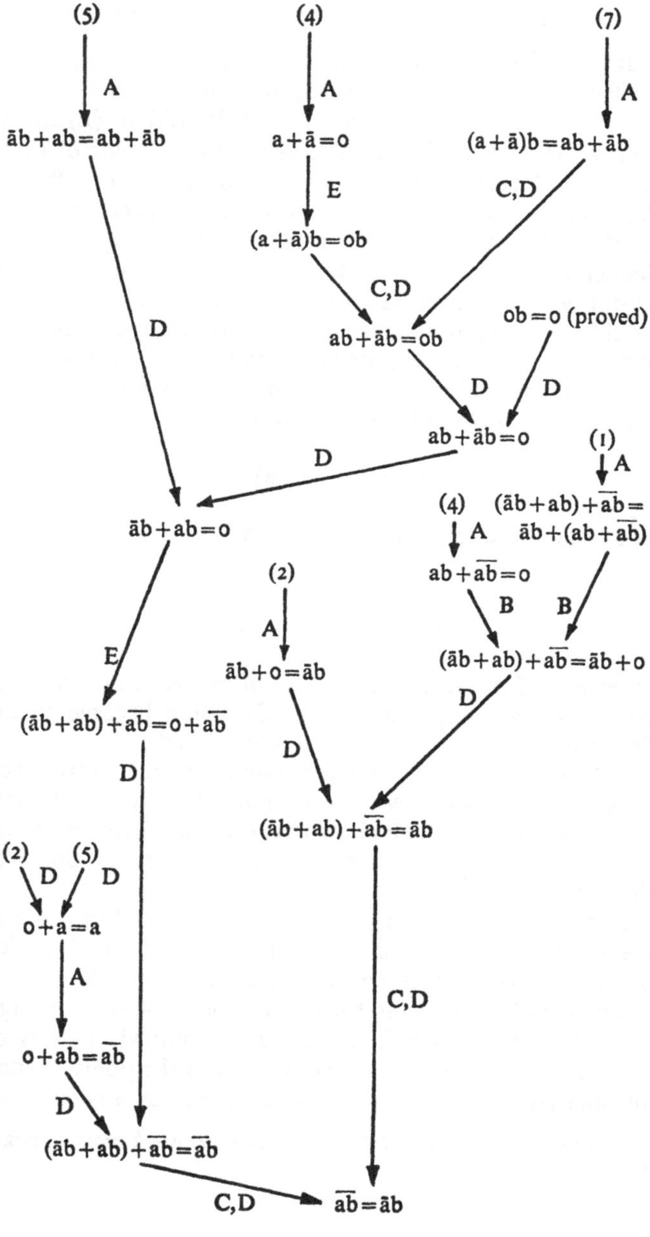

(5)
A
$\bar{a}b+ab=ab+\bar{a}b$
D
(4)
A
$a+\bar{a}=o$
E
$(a+\bar{a})b=ob$
C,D
(7)
A
$(a+\bar{a})b=ab+\bar{a}b$
C,D
$ab+\bar{a}b=ob$
$ob=o$ (proved)
D
D
$ab+\bar{a}b=o$
D
$\bar{a}b+ab=o$
(1)
A
$(\bar{a}b+ab)+\overline{ab}=$
$\bar{a}b+(ab+\overline{ab})$
(4)
A
$ab+\overline{ab}=o$
B
B
$(\bar{a}b+ab)+\overline{ab}=\bar{a}b+o$
D
(2)
A
$\bar{a}b+o=\bar{a}b$
D
E
$(\bar{a}b+ab)+\overline{ab}=o+\overline{ab}$
D
$(\bar{a}b+ab)+\overline{ab}=\bar{a}b$
C,D
(2)
D
(5)
D
$o+a=a$
A
$o+\overline{ab}=\overline{ab}$
D
$(\bar{a}b+ab)+\overline{ab}=\overline{ab}$
C,D
$\overline{ab}=\bar{a}b$

analysis? For hundreds of thousands of years we and our forefathers have been enjoying the fruit grown on the trees of this planet; why do scientists now have to analyse the fruit into its component chemical substances? Partly out of sheer curiosity; but partly because, by knowing the exact structure of fruit, we can take steps to provide adequate substitutes. The reader who is naturally curious about what makes a particular structure what it is will in any case want to delve into the minute logical detail which constitutes mathematical thinking. Further, by becoming aware of what constitutes the mathematical thinking we require of children, we could provide the same sort of mental training for them in a much more systematic way, by requiring them to go through prototype reasoning patterns of progressive complexity. These patterns would at first need to be simpler in structure than the ones already illustrated, whose hidden complexity only begins to be felt when attempts are made to *relate* statements to each other. We thus become aware of the ways in which we habitually link statements in chains, and make explicit the kinds of links that are described in the rules of procedure (A) to (E). It may be quite a salutary shock for us! If, then, we are going to expose children to the rigours of mathematical analysis, perhaps they should be broken in a little more gently. Let us take a somewhat simpler problem.

Which of the statements (1) to (8) do we need, and what kinds of methods of deduction must we use, to prove that $\bar{\bar{a}} = a$?

In (4) replace a by $\bar{a}$, we obtain

$\bar{\bar{a}}+\bar{a}=0$ (using A) .. .. (α)

Now add a on both sides obtaining

$(\bar{\bar{a}}+\bar{a})+a=0+a$ (using E) .. .. (β)

In (1) replace a by $\bar{\bar{a}}$, b by $\bar{a}$ and c by a, we obtain

$(\bar{\bar{a}}+\bar{a})+a=\bar{\bar{a}}+(\bar{a}+a)$ (using A) .. .. .. (γ)

From (β) and (γ) using C and D we have

$$\bar{\bar{a}}+(\bar{a}+a)=0+a \quad \ldots \quad (\delta)$$

Putting $\bar{a}$ for b in (4) we have $\bar{a}+a=0$, which we may put into (δ), also replacing the right-hand side of (δ) by a in virtue of (2), using B in both cases, we obtain

$$\bar{\bar{a}}+0=a \quad \ldots \quad (\epsilon)$$

now putting $\bar{\bar{a}}$ for a in (2) we have,

$$\bar{\bar{a}}+0=\bar{\bar{a}} \text{ (using A)} \quad \ldots \quad (\lambda)$$

and from (ϵ) and (λ) using C and D we obtain

$$\bar{\bar{a}}=a \quad \text{(End formula)}$$

The proof schema could be drawn spatially as shown on page 161.

This is clearly a less complex structure than the proof of the statement (10). The mental mapping of such structures is the stock-in-trade of the practising mathematician. The amazing thing is that, out of all the possible nonsense that he might put together in the first place for eventual analysis, he more often than not makes a correct guess at the end-point and proceeds to fill in the missing parts. This is called making, and then proving, a conjecture.

We have seen that in some cases it is possible to find proof schemata, which establish relationships of dependence between mathematical statements. By looking at the last schema we see that the statement $\bar{\bar{a}}=a$ is dependent on (1), (2) and (4) but not, for example, on (5). We do not need to make use of the commutative property postulated in the statement (5) in order to arrive at $\bar{\bar{a}}=a$. This means that non-commutative structures, as long as they possess the properties expressed in (1), (2) and (4), will have the property that for every element of the structure $\bar{\bar{a}}=a$. We have already come across such structures among the 6-move and the 8-move games studied in the third chapter.

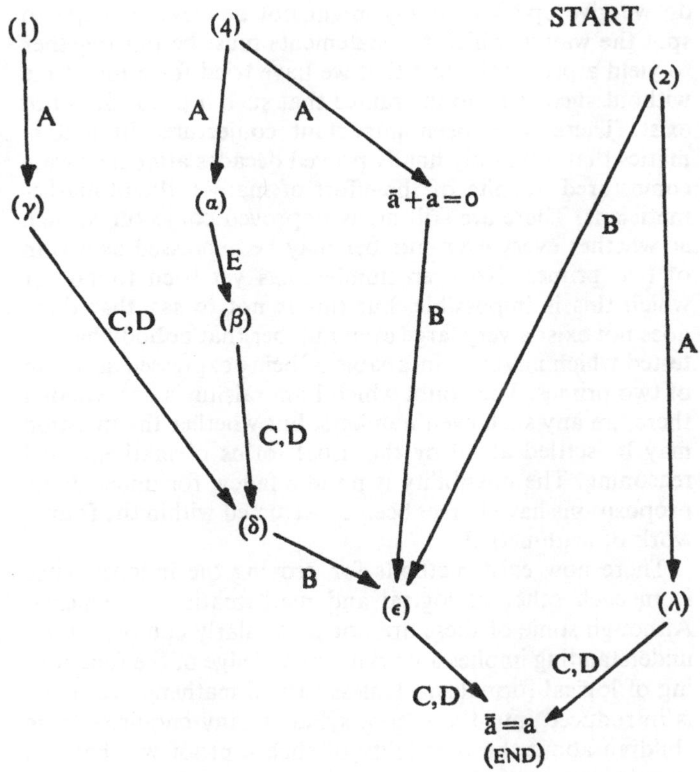

If there are relations of dependence amongst mathematical statements, there are also certain to be relations of independence. This would be the case if a statement were incapable of being proved from a certain set of statements by the admitted rules of procedure. For example, we might wonder whether (5) can be proved by means of some or all of the other statements (1) to (8). If such proof turned out to be impossible, we would say that (5) is independent of the rest of the set (1) to (8). We might go on for a long time trying to find a proof of (5) without success. At what point do we give up? We simply might not be clever enough to spot the way in which the statements must be put together to yield a proof; the fact that we have tried for a long time without success is no guarantee that such a proof does not exist. There have been important conjectures in mathematics that were only finally proved decades after they were conjectured in spite of the effort of many brilliant mathematicians. There are still many unproved conjectures, such as whether every even number may be expressed as a sum of two primes. No even number has yet been found for which this is impossible, but this is not to say that there does not exist a very large even number that nobody has yet tested which might be incapable of being expressed as a sum of two primes. The doubt which I am raising is not whether there are any such even numbers, but whether the question may be settled at all by the usual forms of mathematical reasoning. The possibility is no idle fancy, for undecidable propositions have in fact been constructed within the framework of arithmetic.[1]

There now exist methods for proving the independence from each other of logical and mathematical statements. Although some of these are not particularly complex, their understanding implies a working knowledge of the functioning of logical formalism. Unless formal mathematical logic is introduced into the school syllabus, any enquiries from children about the possibility of such a proof will have to remain unanswered.

Initial statements which are taken as starting points in a proof within a system are usually called axioms. The statements (1) to (8) are axioms which characterize mathematical structures known as *rings*. The statements (1) to (4) characterize mathematical structures known as *groups*. All these statements are independent of each other, and can serve as a tidy set of axioms for these structures ('tidy' in the sense that no statement is redundant; that is, deducible from the rest of the statements). Examples of groups have been

[1] See Volume II of *Grundlagen der Mathematik* (Hilbert and Bernays). First such statement constructed by Kurt Gödel in 1932

given in the third chapter. The integers form a ring with addition as first operation and multiplication as second operation. The even integers also form a ring, but the odd integers do not. The set of all polynomials with whole number coefficients also forms a ring. The reader might like to decide whether the set of elements α, β forms a ring under the following rules of composition for the two operations:

$$\alpha+\alpha=\alpha,\ \alpha+\beta=\beta,\ \beta+\alpha=\beta,\ \beta+\beta=\alpha \text{ and}$$
$$\alpha\alpha=\alpha,\quad \alpha\beta=\alpha,\quad \beta\alpha=\alpha,\quad \beta\beta=\beta.$$

To compare structures which are characterized by the same set of axioms is the mathematician's way of discarding unnecessary trimmings which may still adhere to their images. Having come across, possibly without knowing it, many exemplars of groups, he has to decide what it is that all these exemplars have in common. This set of properties will be a kind of outer shell into which they all fit. The axioms (1), (2), (3) and (4) are this outer shell, together with the rules of procedure about obtaining other statements from the axioms. The most abstract definition of a group is the axiomatic one, namely that any structure with any elements in which a binary operation is defined is a group, as long as these elements and this operation satisfy the axioms (1) to (4). A ring is any structure with any elements with two binary operations defined, where the elements and the operations satisfy the axioms (1) to (8).

Strictly speaking, another 'closure' axiom should be added to the definition of a ring, namely

(3) To every pair of numbers a, b, corresponds a number c such that a.b = c.

Incidentally, in all the axioms the word 'number' should really be replaced by the word 'element', unless 'number' is taken in a much wider sense than is customary among mathematicians.

It will be appreciated that adding more axioms to a system makes certain structures ineligible. For example, adding axiom (5) excludes all non-commutative structures.

Adding axioms (6), (7) and (8) selects among the mathematical groups those that are also rings. We may add more axioms to our ring axioms, and so obtain a system that characterizes such structures as the rational numbers, real numbers or complex numbers. We may add the following:

(U) There is an element, denoted by e or by 1, which is such that for every element a we have $a.1 = a = 1.a$ (in other words there exists a unit element)

(D) To every element a, different from 0, corresponds an element b such that

$$a.b = b.a = 1$$

Such an element is usually denoted $b = a^{-1}$.

Any structure satisfying (1) to (8) as well as (U) is called a *ring with unity*, any structure satisfying (1) to (8) as well as (U) and (D) is called a *field*. It will be verified that the positive and negative integers form a ring with unity, the even integers (positive and negative) a ring without unity, addition and multiplication being the two operations. The rational numbers, both real numbers and complex numbers, form fields. There are fields which are more extensive than the rational numbers but do not include all real numbers. For example, numbers that can be written as

$$a + \sqrt{2}.b$$

where a and b are rational numbers form such a field.

We may like to add another axiom, that of the commutativity of the second operation, i.e.

(C) For every element a and b, $a.b = b.a$.

It will have been noted that in axiom (D) an exception had to be introduced about the existence of the inverse element with respect to the second operation. This is because it has been proved that in any ring

$$a.0 = 0.a = 0$$

for any element a of the ring. This implies that o could not have an inverse, as if it did, we should have

$$0.0^{-1} = 1$$

and there would be an element, namely 0^{-1}, which would contradict the theorem o.a = o. So an element 0^{-1} could not exist. But for this fact, the axiom (3′), (6), (U), and (D) would define a group, where the binary operation was the second operation. If, on the other hand, we consider all the elements of the ring but exclude o, these axioms do define a group.

The study of groups, rings and fields in mathematics is an attempt to kill several birds with one stone. Having studied the properties of rings, we have already, unwittingly, studied the properties of polynomials, of finite decimals, of certain types of transformations and so on. The axiomatic study of structures takes in a great number of structures at the same time, abstracting from these structures everything except the properties expressed in the axioms. Great economy of effort is achieved in this way, not to mention the important insights obtained through a meticulous examination and analysis of what certain types of structures are really made of.

In the fourth chapter the properties of vector spaces were built up through the use of imagined situations so structured as to be exemplars of a 'vector space'. After playing about with these structures to see what they will and will not do, to complete the mathematical thought cycle we could analyse the properties that characterize a vector space. This will make us more consciously aware of them, so that we shall be more likely to recognize a vector space in future.

The elements in a vector space are vectors. Let us denote these by letters A, B, C, . . . etc. There is a binary operation defined, so that to every pair of vectors corresponds a vector, usually called the sum of the two vectors in the pair. We could write for example

$$A + B = C$$

It is also evident that the associative law holds in all the exemplars we have come across of vector spaces, and the theorem proved on transformations confirms this fact. We can express it symbolically as

$$(A+B)+C=A+(B+C)$$

There is also a 'zero vector' which, added to any vector, leaves that vector unaltered. We can symbolize this by saying that

$$O+A=A+O=A$$

To every vector there has always been an 'opposite' vector; if we add these together we obtain the zero vector. Using a bar to denote 'the opposite of', we can symbolize the above by saying:

To every vector A there is a vector $\bar{A}$ such that

$$A+\bar{A}=\bar{A}+A=O$$

The four properties thus developed are in fact the group properties. We can say that the vectors in a vector space form a group, the binary operation being vector addition.

During our study of vector spaces we considered multiples of vectors by directed numbers. If we wish to include fractions, we can say in our new terminology that we allow multiplications by elements of a field. We need to introduce the following new axioms to deal with such multiplications, where a, b, . . . are elements of a field, and A, B, . . . are vectors in the vector space:

(V_1) $(a+b)A=aA+bA$,
(V_2) $a(A+B)=aA+aB$,
(V_3) $a(bA)=(ab)A$,
(V_4) $1A=A$, where 1 is the unit element in the field.

It is usual also to add the requirement of commutativity for vector addition, so that our final requirement will be

$$\text{(C)} \qquad A+B=B+A$$

for all vectors A and B in the vector space.

It will be seen that a vector space is quite a different breed of mathematical creature from a ring or a field, and yet all are obtained from groups by adding further requirements. A vector space, a ring and a field are all groups, but they each have something else besides, which is peculiar to themselves. The peculiarity is provided by the extra axioms. To make a ring out of a group, a further binary operation has to be introduced which is associative, and it must be distributive with respect to the first operation. To make a vector space out of a group a field must be found first, and the elements of this field and of the original group must be combined together in such a way as to satisfy the axioms (V_1), (V_2), (V_3), (V_4), (C). This is much more of a hybrid creature than the ring, the ring having only one type of element in it. A field is a more particular creature than a ring, and its two operations must fulfil more requirements than the two operations of the ring.

In the axiomatic definition of a vector space nothing is said about the structure of a vector. The vectors are the final atoms out of which the vector space is constructed, and the relationship between the field and the vectors normally only becomes apparent in the axioms (V_1) to (V_4). This is not quite so if the vector space is constructed out of its vectors. Suppose that we have a field already constructed, we can define a four-dimensional vector as an ordered quadruple of elements of this field, such as might be written in the form

$$(x_1, x_2, x_3, x_4)=X$$

where x_1, x_2, x_3 and x_4 are elements of the field. Instead of *defining* vector addition as any binary operation which satisfies the axioms (1) to (4), as we should do in the axiomatic approach, we could say that by definition if

$$X=(x_1, x_2, x_3, x_4) \text{ and } Y=(y_1, y_2, y_3, y_4) \quad \text{then}$$
$$X+Y=(x_1+y_1, x_2+y_2, x_3+y_3, x_4+y_4);$$

also if c is any element of the field, we could say that by definition

$$cX=(cx_1, cx_2, cx_3, cx_4)$$

for any vector X. It is easily shown that the group axioms are satisfied by such vectors, as we know that the field axioms are satisfied by the 'components'. For example there is a vector (O, O, O, O) which is such that for every vector (x_1, x_2, x_3, x_4) we have

$$(O, O, O, O)+(x_1, x_2, x_3, x_4)=(x_1, x_2, x_3, x_4)$$

and similarly the other three group axioms can be proved to hold from the fact that the 'components' satisfy the field axioms.

It is also easy to prove the axioms (V_1) to (V_4). For example to show that (V_3) holds, we can see that we can write

$$\begin{aligned} a(bX) &= a(bx_1, bx_2, bx_3, bx_4) \\ &= (abx_1, abx_2, abx_3, abx_4) = (ab)X \\ &\quad \text{[using the associative property of the field]} \end{aligned}$$

with similar considerations for the other three axioms. The mathematical entities (x_1, x_2, x_3, x_4), together with the members a, b, c, . . . of the associated field, satisfy all the axioms for a vector space. It would not have made any difference if we had chosen entities like $(x_1, x_2, x_3, x_4, x_5, x_6, x_7)$ as our 'vectors' with similar definitions for the composition laws. In fact, there is nothing in the axioms to stop us from considering an infinite number of components in the brackets. Our axiomatic definition embraces a larger number of entities than those from which we might have abstracted the axiom system to describe the essential relevant properties of these entities. If we find that we have overdone things a little, and have included among the structures satisfying our axiom system structures we had no intention of including, we can always have second thoughts and join another axiom or so to eliminate the unwanted structures.

If we wish to exclude all vector spaces with more than four dimensions, we could state the following additional requirement:

(V_5) To any five vectors X_1, X_2, X_3, X_4, X_5 in the vector space it is always possible to find five field-elements a_1, a_2, a_3, a_4 and a_5 not all of which are the 0 element, such that

$$a_1X_1+a_2X_2+a_3X_3+a_4X_4+a_5X_5$$

is the zero vector.

For example, cubic polynomials form a four-dimensional vector space, as is easily verified by checking the axioms and by proving that if X_1, X_2, X_3, X_4 and X_5 are any five cubic polynomials, numbers a_1, a_2, a_3, a_4 and a_5 can be found, not all zero, such that

$$a_1X_1+a_2X_2+a_3X_3+a_4X_4+a_5X_5$$

is identically zero. The reader who is familiar with the theory of determinants as applied to linear dependence and independence will find no difficulty in this.

In the second part of the fourth chapter, structures described as algebras were built up out of vector spaces. It will be instructive to investigate the axiomatic structure of these constructions, so that their relations to other constructions become clearer. We have seen that a vector space is described by the axioms (1) to (4) and (V_1) to (V_4), together with a dimension axiom, should we wish to restrict the number of possible dimensions in the spaces that satisfy our axioms. To turn a vector space into an algebra, we need to define a multiplication of a vector by a vector, where this multiplication would be associative and distributive with respect to addition. This means joining axioms (6), (7) and (8) to the system; it is also usual to require (5) to hold for addition (i.e. the first operation). In our new terminology, we have extended the group defined by (1), (2), (3), (4), to a ring. We also require associativity between field-elements and vectors for multiplication,

$$(A_1) \qquad (aA)B = a(AB) = A(aB)$$

From this is is easy to prove that

$$(aA)(bB) = (ab)(AB)$$

It should be stated perhaps that axiom (V_5) does not ensure that all spaces satisfying the axioms with the addition of (V_5) will be four-dimensional. It merely ensures that they will not be more than four-dimensional. To make sure that only exactly four-dimensional spaces satisfy the axioms, we should have to add that there exist in the space four vectors, U_1, U_2, U_3 and U_4; that none of these is the zero vector; and that, however we may try to combine them to obtain the zero vector by requiring

$$a_1U_1 + a_2U_2 + a_3U_3 + a_4U_4 = 0$$

(a_1, a_2, a_3, a_4 being field-elements), the *only* way of making sure that this is so is by choosing all the elements to be zero. In the language of linear algebra, we are requiring the existence of at least four linearly independent vectors in the space, but not more than four (as required by the present (V_5)).

If there exist four vectors U_1, U_2, U_3, and U_4 as required by the further restriction on axiom (V_5), then in virtue of axiom (V_5), X being any given non-zero vector, there must exist a non-zero field-element *a* such that

$$a\,X + a_1U_1 + a_2U_2 + a_3U_3 + a_4U_4 = 0$$

where at least one of a_1, a_2, a_3, a_4 must be different from zero. It is easy to see that a cannot be zero, because if it were, then

$$a_1U_1+a_2U_2+a_3U_3+a_4U_4$$

would be the zero vector, which would entail by restriction on (V_5) that

$$a_1=a_2=a_3=a_4=0$$

If a can only be zero, then there are five vectors in the space which can only be combined linearly by zero coefficients to obtain the zero vector, which contradicts axiom (V_5). Since $a\neq 0$, as a is in a field, a^{-1} exists, and $a^{-1}a=1$, and $1.X=X$. Multiplying both sides of (1) on the left by a^{-1}, we have

$$X=\alpha_1U_1+\alpha_2U_2+\alpha_3U_3+{}_4\alpha U_4$$

where the field-elements $\alpha_1,\alpha_2,\alpha_3,\alpha_4$ are not all zero. We have shown that every vector in the space is expressible linearly in terms of U_1, U_2, U_3, U_4. The vector X could be written as $(\alpha_1, \alpha_2, \alpha_3, \alpha_4)$ and the vectors U_1, U_2, U_3, U_4 as

$$(1, 0, 0, 0), (0, 1, 0, 0), (0, 0, 1, 0), (0, 0, 0, 1)$$

respectively. The vectors U_1, U_2, U_3, U_4 may be termed the 'unit vectors' in the co-ordinate system defined by these vectors. We have shown that the restricted dimension axiom, when added to the axioms (1) to (4) and (V_1) to (V_4), will yield only the kinds of constructions described earlier.

The distributive laws postulated in (7) and (8) entail that

$$\text{if } X=a_1U_1+a_2U_2+a_3U_3+a_4U_4 \quad \text{and}$$
$$Y=b_1U_1+b_2U_2+b_3U_3+b_4U_4$$

then

$$\begin{aligned} XY=&a_1b_1U_1U_1+a_1b_2U_1U_2+a_1b_3U_1U_3+a_1a_4U_1U_4\\ &+a_2b_1U_2U_1+a_2b_2U_2U_2+a_2b_3U_2U_3+a_2b_4U_2U_4\\ &+a_3b_1U_3U_1+a_3b_2U_3U_2+a_3b_3U_3U_3+a_3b_4U_3U_4\\ &+a_4b_1U_4U_1+a_4b_2U_4U_2+a_4b_3U_4U_3+a_4b_4U_4U_4\end{aligned}$$

and the definition of multiplication, i.e. of the second operation in the ring into which we extend the group constituting the vector space, will consist of deciding what the products of the unit vectors U_iU_j are going to be for values of i and j between 1 and 4 inclusive. Since any vector is expressible in terms of the unit vectors, we must decide for every product

$$U_iU_j = \beta_{ij1}U_1 + \beta_{ij2}U_2 + \beta_{ij3}U_3 + \beta_{ij4}U_4$$

what the field-elements β_{ijk} are going to be. In the four-dimensional case this means deciding on 64 values; in the n-dimensional case, deciding on n^3 values for the coefficients.

The complex algebra is built up out of the two-dimensional vector space with unit vectors $U_1 = (1, 0)$ and $U_2 = (0, 1)$ by the following four definitions for the products of the unit vectors:

$$U_1U_1 = 1U_1 + 0U_2;\ U_1U_2 = 0U_1 + 1U_2;$$
$$U_2U_1 = 0U_1 + 1U_2;\ U_2U_2 = \bar{1}U_1 + 0U_2$$

where 1 is the unit element in the field of real numbers and $\bar{1}$ its additive inverse. The $2^3 = 8$ coefficients determining the algebra are here

$$a_{111} = 1, \quad a_{112} = 0, \quad a_{121} = 0, \quad a_{122} = 1,$$
$$a_{211} = 0, \quad a_{212} = 1, \quad a_{221} = \bar{1}, \quad a_{222} = 0$$

This is what was referred to as the second structure in the fourth chapter. The first structure only differs from the second in the value of the coefficient a_{221} which is 1 instead of $\bar{1}$. It is interesting that such a small alteration in the axiomatic definition of a structure could make such a difference to its properties; the first structure has zero divisors and the second one has not.

It will be instructive to analyse in a similar fashion one or two other algebraic structures, for example the three-dimensional dance story on page 116. If the unit vectors are

U_1, U_2, and U_3 represented in the story by boy, teenage boy and man respectively, then their additive inverses are $\bar{1}U_1$, $\bar{1}U_2$ and $\bar{1}U_3$, which are girl, teenage girl and woman in the story. The multiplications of the unit vectors are defined as follows:

$$U_1U_1=U_1,\ U_1U_2=U_2,\ U_1U_3=U_3;$$
$$U_2U_1=U_2,\ U_2U_2=U_3,\ U_2U_3=\bar{1}U_1;$$
$$U_3U_1=U_3,\ U_3U_2=\bar{1}U_1;\ U_3U_3=\bar{1}U_2$$

and the $3^3=27$ coefficients defining the algebra are given by

$$a_{111}=1,\ a_{112}=0,\ a_{113}=0,\ a_{121}=0,\ a_{122}=1,\ a_{123}=0,$$
$$a_{131}=0,\ a_{132}=0,\ a_{133}=1,\ a_{211}=0,\ a_{212}=1,\ a_{213}=0,$$
$$a_{221}=0,\ a_{222}=0,\ a_{223}=1,\ a_{231}=\bar{1},\ a_{232}=0,\ a_{233}=0,$$
$$a_{311}=0,\ a_{312}=0,\ a_{313}=1,\ a_{321}=\bar{1},\ a_{322}=0,\ a_{323}=0,$$
$$a_{331}=0,\ a_{332}=\bar{1},\ a_{333}=0.$$

Of course, there is no need for so many coefficients to be zero. In fact, it would be possible to define an algebra which was isomorphic to the above by taking a non-degenerate 3-by-3 transformation such as

$$V_i=\beta_{i1}U_1+\beta_{i2}U_2+\beta_{i3}U_3 \text{ for } i=1, 2\ 3$$

whose inverse can then be computed and written as

$$U_i=\alpha_{i1}V_1+\alpha_{i2}V_2+\alpha_{i3}V_3 \text{ for } i=1, 2, 3$$

The products V_iV_j may then be calculated in terms of U_1, U_2, U_3, using the table of values for U_iU_j for doing so. Expressions for U_1, U_2 and U_3 can then be substituted in terms of V_1, V_2 and V_3 from the inverse transformation, which will give a new set of 27 values for ijk, defining another, apparently more complicated, algebra. If the algebra based on (U_1, U_2, U_3) was for example commutative, the algebra based on (V_1, V_2, V_3) will likewise be commutative. Each algebra will be an image of the other; if we denote by T the transformation of a vector from the first algebra into the second, it will be found that

$$\mathrm{T(X)+T(Y)=T(X+Y)} \quad \text{and}$$
$$\mathrm{T(X).T(Y)=T(X.Y)}$$

An example on which to try this first would come better from a two-dimensional structure like the complex algebra, so that the computations are reduced to a minimum. Let U_1 and U_2 denote the fundamental unit vectors in the complex algebra, those usually denoted by 1 and i. Consider the following transformation:

$$V_1=2U_1+1U_2 \qquad U_1=2V_1+\bar{1}V_2$$
and its inverse
$$V_2=3U_1+2U_2 \qquad U_2=\bar{3}V_1+2V_2$$

Using the fundamental defining relationships of the algebra, i.e.

$$U_1U_1=U_1,\ U_1U_2=U_2,$$
$$U_2U_1=U_2,\ U_2U_2=\bar{1}U_1$$

we obtain

$$V_1V_1=3U_1+4U_2=\bar{6}V_1+5V_2$$
$$V_1V_2=V_2V_1=4U_1+7U_2=\overline{13}V_1+10V_2$$
$$V_2V_2=5U_1+12U_2=\overline{26}V_1+19V_2$$

This means that the defining coefficients of the algebra from the field of real numbers are the following eight numbers:

$$\beta_{111}=\bar{6}, \quad \beta_{112}=5, \quad \beta_{121}=\overline{13}, \quad \beta_{122}=10,$$
$$\beta_{211}=\overline{13}, \quad \beta_{212}=10, \quad \beta_{221}=\overline{26}, \quad \beta_{222}=19$$

We may check that $2V_1+\bar{1}V_2$ is the unit element in the ring so defined; that is to say, that multiplication by this vector will leave any vector unaltered, assuming that we follow through the multiplication rules for the new unit vectors V_1 and V_2 as given above in the expressions for V_iV_j.

Or a check may be made on relations like

$$(U_1+U_2).(U_1+\bar{1}U_2)=2U_1$$

Carrying out the necessary substitutions we obtain in fact

$$\begin{aligned}(U_1+U_2).(U_1+\bar{1}U_2)&=(\bar{1}V_1+V_2).(5V_1+\bar{3}V_2)\\&=4V_1+\bar{2}V_2=2.(2V_1+\bar{1}V_2)\\&=2U_1\end{aligned}$$

We have taken $X=U_1+U_2$, $Y=U_1+\bar{1}U_2$, and we have $T(X)=\bar{1}V_1+V_2$ and $T(Y)=5V_1+\bar{3}V_2$, and $XY=2U_1$ and $T(XY)=4V_1+\bar{2}V_2$.
We have also seen that $T(X).T(Y)$ turns out to be $4V_1+\bar{2}V_2$. So in this case at least

$$T(X.Y)=T(X).T(Y)$$

This kind of analytical playing with the axiomatic structure of algebras brings up the question of how to prove such statements about algebras and their transformations. By axiomatizing the constructions we have built up, we have laid bare their essential structures, and have provided a most powerful tool of investigation. The playing about at this stage is truly mathematical, and the variability principles will now become less and less necessary. We shall learn better and better the art of handling structures as 'outer shells' or 'grey images' or 'extracted essences', putting these structures under the analytical microscope whose essence is the axiomatic method.

Precisely *when* children become mature enough to be safely exposed to the chill winds of such mathematical rigour we have yet to find out. It is clearly not advisable to begin the study of a structure by an axiomatic statement of its properties; as we have seen, the more natural process is to become familiar with the structure, and with similar structures, by playing about with them to see how they behave. It is only after extensive playing of rule-bound games that children will raise the analytic questions which lead to axiomatic considerations. But so few children in the world today are building up any kind of sound mathematical structures that it will not be easy to discover when and under what circumstances they can appreciate and understand an axiomatic treatment of a structure. The symbolic constructions, such as those suggested for vector spaces, are probably a necessary intermediate stage between playing by the rules and the axiomatization of the rules.

We have travelled the long and difficult road from play to the rigour of truly mathematical reasoning. We have followed this road across the mathematical country of groups, rings, fields, vector spaces and algebras, and tried to suggest various ways in which children can make use of constructions, games, imagination, and the fashioning of tools such as symbolic language and finally the tool of axiomatics. It goes without saying that mathematics is immensely wider than the glimpses that have been given of it in these pages, even the mathematics that children in schools could understand if only they were given the chance to explore it under the guidance of sympathetic and enthusiastic teachers. I hope that what I have said will contribute to the now world-wide rethinking of the problems of learning and of teaching mathematics in schools, and help to make the mathematics lesson a happier and more exciting event.